Marked

Poems of the Holocaust

Marked

Poems of the Holocaust

Stephen Herz

NᴑY Books™

The New York Quarterly Foundation, Inc.
New York, New York

NYQ Books™ is an imprint of The New York Quarterly Foundation, Inc.

The New York Quarterly Foundation, Inc.
P. O. Box 2015
Old Chelsea Station
New York, NY 10113

www.nyq.org

First Edition

Set in New Baskerville

Layout and Design by Raymond P. Hammond
Cover Design by Howard Friedman

The cover image of the yellow, cloth star is from the United States Holocaust Memorial Museum Collection, Gift of Klaus M. Zwilsky and is gratefully used here with permission.

Library of Congress Control Number: 2014931067

ISBN: 978-1-935520-79-5

Marked

Poems of the Holocaust

Acknowledgments

Grateful acknowledgment is made to the editors of the following publications in which several of these poems appeared, some in slightly different form: *Amelia, American Poetry Monthly, Barbaric Yawp, Barnwood, Black Bear Review, Blue Unicorn, Bogg, Boulevard, Clackamus Review, Comstock Review, Connecticut Review, Connecticut River Review, Green Fuse, Hollins Critic, The Jewish Ledger, The Larcom Review, The Ledge, Nedge, The New York Quarterly, Parnassus, Parting Gifts, Plainsongs, Poem, Poets On, Poets Page, Prism, Sheila-Na-Gig, Small Pond, Southern Poetry Review, This, Whiskey Island Magazine,* and *Wind.*

Marked, this second collection of my Holocaust poems, includes nearly all the poems—some slightly revised—from *Whatever You Can Carry* Barnwood Press, 2003. Some poems previously appeared in chapbooks also titled *Whatever You Can Carry* from New School University, 1996, and Pudding House, 2000. The poems "Marked," "Jedwabne," "Shot," "In Your Lager Dream," and "Fried Noodles Topped with Raisins Cinnamon and Vanilla Cream" were published in the anthology *Blood To Remember: American Poets On The Holocaust,* Time Being Books, 2007. *Whatever You Can Carry* is in the archives of the United States Holocaust Memorial Museum in Washington, DC.

With thanks to Erica Kaplan and Howard Friedman and my editor Raymond Hammond. And with remembrance to my mentors Pearl London and Jason Shinder. And a belated thanks to Thomas Lux for his help and encouragement for many of these poems.

Contents

Part One: The Jew Is Your Enemy

Part Four: The Dead & Dying

"The yellow star?
      Oh well, what of it? You don't die of it?"
Poor Father!
      Of what then did you die?

—Elie Wiesel

The vast majority wore the star
      and wearing it were lost.

—Raul Hilberg

For all those dead burnt bodies
and all those yellow stars
in anonymous graves
who can't speak for themselves.

Part One: The Jew Is Your Enemy

Found Poem

(circa 1930–45)

The Jew is your eternal enemy.
The Jew is a cheat, he is your only enemy.
The Jew pulls the strings.
The Jew carries the louse and typhus.
The Jew is money-mad bits of filth.
The Jew is devoid of all higher values,
      corrupters of the world.
The Jew directs the actions of Churchill,
      Roosevelt and Stalin.
The Jew is behind the Marxist United Front.
The Jew is vermin.
The Jew is behind the Pope's representatives.
The Jew does not belong among you,
      drive him out.
The Jews profit from Christmas holidays.
The Jews are instigators of Bolshevism.
The Jews are a great clique of criminals.
The Jews will hang.
The Jewish cattle-dealer ruins the peasants.
The Jewish international high finance
      drinks the blood of nations.
The Jewish people stand against us as our
      deadly foe.
The Jew is your enemy: whoever buys from
      the Jew is a traitor to his people.
The Jews of the whole world are trying to
      destroy Germany.
The Jew is responsible for the war.
The Jew is your enemy: Sow Jew. Filth Jew.
      Stink Jew.
The Jews are undoubtedly a race, but they
      are not human.

Burning the Books
to Purify German Culture

When one burns books,
one will in the end burn people.
—Heinrich Heine

Throughout Nazi Germany,
starting on the night of May 10, 1933
hundreds of thousands of books
"of noxious Jewish writings and non-Jews
suspected of writing in the Jewish spirit"
were thrown onto bonfires by angry
and exhilarated mobs—many of them students.

Albert Einstein, Sigmund Freud,
Stefan Zweig, Thomas Mann, Bertolt Brecht,
Franz Wegel, Erich Maria Remarque,
Max Brod, Jack London, Ernest Hemingway,
Upton Sinclair, John Dos Passos,
Theodore Dreiser, Sinclair Lewis…

In Berlin 20,000 books were burned.
The public burnings were accompanied
by torchlight parades, dancing, chants,
and massive bonfires. As the books went
up in flames they gave the Nazi salute.

Franz Boas, Karl Marx, V.I. Lenin,
Leon Trotsky, Rosa Luxember, H.G. Wells,
Dr. Magnus Hirschfeld, Margaret Sanger,
Eric Baron, Helen Keller, Alfred Döblin,
Carl von Ossietzky, Kurt Tucholsk,
Hugo von Ossietzk, Eric Kästner…

"The age of hairsplitting
Jewish intellectualism
is dead…the past lies in flames,"
said Joseph Goebbels.

Carl Zuckmayer, Arnold Zweig,
Jacob Wassermann, Theodore Wolf,
Anna Seghers, Hans Marchwitza, Jose Roth,
Professor Grossmann, Erwin Kisch,
Heinz Pol, Bernard Kellermann,
Vici Baum, Adrienne Thome,
George Kaiser...

Time called it a "bibliocaust."
Newsweek called it "a holocaust of books."

All Jews

All Jews
must take an additional
middle name:
every man *Israel*
every woman *Sara*

☆

All Jews
over age 15
must apply for identity cards
to be shown on demand
to any police officer—
Jewish passports
must be stamped
with a large red J

☆

All Jews
six years or over
are to appear in public
only when wearing
the Jewish star,
the star must be as large
as the palm of a hand,
must be sewn
to the left front of clothing,
its color, black,
background, yellow
in the center
a black
Jude

The Old Hatred

on our windows
        the yellow star

the crooked cross
        of swastika—

on our windows
        the old hatred

Jude
    Jew Pig
        Die Jew

glass breaking
        breaking

our Torahs, bibles,
        synagogues

burning, burning.

On the night of November 9, 1938, violence broke out against the Jews throughout the Reich. In forty-eight hours over a thousand synagogues were burned, seven thousand Jewish businesses were trashed and looted, ninety-six Jews were killed, Jewish cemeteries, hospitals, schools and homes were destroyed, and thirty thousand Jews were sent to concentration camps. The Germans called the pogrom Kristallnacht—night of broken glass. It marked the start of the Holocaust.

Two Days After *Kristallnacht*

I would like
to say

that I would
not

like to be
a Jew

in Germany.

November 12, 1938—Herman Goering charging the Jews must pay 1 billion Reichmarks for the damages after Kristallnacht.

Thanksgiving, 1938

"That Hitler, he's worse than the Kaiser,
he's up to no good," says my grandfather.
"I heard him on the Philco, he sure likes
to shout," I say.

"Your father's some carver," my mother says.
"I mean just look how he gets right in there,
just like a surgeon, I mean just look at those
slices of white meat coming off so thin.

I hate thick. Like my cranberries? I made
them the way your father likes them.
Strained. Nice and tart. And I always get
sweet potatoes, not yams. Sweet potatoes are

so much, well, sweeter, don't you think?"
"What do you think about the new Dodge?"
asks Uncle Lee. "What do you think about
the New Deal?" asks Uncle Harry.

"What do you think about the synagogues,
burning? All those synagogues, all those
Torahs, all that glass breaking in the stores.
Next thing they'll be burning Jews.

I wrote my brother: 'Ludwig, get out of
Oppenheim, get out of Germany,
before soon you won't anymore be able.'
So what do you think?" asks my grandfather.

"It'll pass, I think it'll pass,
it usually does," says my father.
"Do you think you can pass me some more dark,
and some white?" I ask.

"We got a new toastmaster," my sister says,
"and it pops right up,
and you never even have to turn the toast.
It's automatic."

To Stay Alive—
The *Kindertransports*

"to stay alive
you have to leave—

you're going to England,
you'll be safe there—

we will follow you,"
they said.

so they packed you
a small suitcase

& you took your doll—
they said goodbye quickly

& put you on the
Kindertransport—

you cried
& you came to England—

you were lucky
your foster family

clothed and fed you
& made you

a part of the family.

you learned the language
& you waited

weeks, months, days
for the thinning mail—

& then nothing.

On December 1, 1938, three weeks after Kristallnacht, the first 200 children left Berlin on the Kindertransport. In the following months, 10,000 unaccompanied mostly Jewish children from Germany, Austria, Poland & Czechoslovakia traveled to England—they were saved, but most would never see their parents again.

S.S. St. Louis Sailing Off Florida Coast
with Cargo of Unwanted

America, we can see the lights of Miami.
America, we're nine hundred and seven Jews fleeing
        Hitler.
America, we're nine hundred and seven human beings
        looking for a haven.
America, they won't let us land in Cuba.
America, you won't let us land in America.
America, we're cabling you:
        How can you be silent? Help!
America, have you forgotten
        Emma Lazarus's words of hope on your
        Statue of Liberty?
America, why have your Jews forgotten us?
America, where is FDR?
America, is it true Henry Ford has a sign on his plant:
        Jews Destroy Christianity
        Jews Control The Press
        Jews Produce Filthy Movies.
America, are you anti-Semitic?
America, some of us are committing suicide.
America, your quota numbers will never reach us in time.
America, the lights of Miami are fading
        into yellow stars.

At sea for over a month, the St. Louis docked in Antwerp June, 1939. France, Great Britain, Holland and Belgium granted the Jews temporary haven. England was the only safe refuge. Many of the others were murdered in Auschwitz and Sobibor. Some went into hiding, some survived, a few succeeded in emigrating to the U.S. before 1945.

That Cursed Race

going to work or school is *verboten*.
eating in a restaurant is *verboten*.

going to the theater, movie, or soccer match is *verboten*.
riding the trams is *verboten*.

green grass and your favorite park bench are *verboten*.
sidewalks are *verboten*:

you must walk in the middle of the road
wearing your yellow star,

the star that marks you *Jude*,
marks you so everyone is watching,

marks you alone, the other, the stranger,
marks you for your friend who writes:

I can no longer be your friend
because you come from that cursed race.

The Jews Are Our Misfortune

Die Juden sind unser Unglück
The Jews are our misfortune

Deutschland erwach
Germany awake

Juda verrecke!
death to Judah!

We Raise Our Right Arm
Give the Nazi Salute

Heil Hitler

Heil Mein Führer

Hitler: Sieg Heil

The Nazi salute was mandatory for all civilians.

Defending Myself
Against the Jew

I believe that
I am acting
in accordance
with the will of
the Almighty Creator
defending myself against the Jew,
I am fighting for the work
of the Lord.

Adolf Hitler, Mein Kampf.

You Jews
Aren't the Same People
Anymore

we who have Jewish friends

who work for Jews

who go together to the coffeehouses
with Jews

who play football with Jews

all of a sudden

you Jews
aren't the same people anymore—

you dirty Jews
sooner or later we're going

to kill you all.

Singing Brownshirts

Wenn das Judenblut vom Messer Spritz
*dann geht's noch mal so gut.**

When Jewish blood drips from the knife
then things are twice as good.

Der Stürmer
The Attacker

attacking Jews in a weekly tabloid
 with antisemitic caricatures
& atrocities & articles demanding
 the annihilation of the Jewish race—

Der Stürmer
 Jews as snakes & spiders.

Der Stürmer
 Jews with large hooked noses
  short, fat, with piglike bulging eyes.

Der Stürmer
 Jews as "Satan" in league with the devil.

Der Stürmer
 partially naked women as victims
  of the Jews.

Der Stürmer
 Jews extracting blood from
  Christian children.

Der Stürmer
 on its front page, the motto—

Die Juden sind unser Unglück!
 The Jews are our misfortune!

Der Stürmer
 Hitler praising it—

Now Jews are known
 for what they are.

Julius Streicher, the editor & publisher of Der Stürmer, was tried at Nuremberg for his role in inciting Germans to exterminate Jews. He was found guilty and hung on October 16, 1946.

Message from the Camp

Your husband
has died of a heart attack.
We will send you an urn
with his ashes.
For this send us
three marks and a half.

Anything But Jewish

when you hear German
look the other way

you must not talk
you must not pee in front of other boys

you must live as a gentile
among gentiles

trust no one outside
your foster family

forget your mother
forget your father

forget your name
forget your yellow star

say you are Protestant
say you are Catholic

say you are anything
but Jewish.

Burned

The first days
of
the

German
advance

into
Polish
cities

they
set
fire

to the
Jewish
sections

shot
dead

Jews
who
ran

from
the burning
buildings

the rabbi
in
Widawa

was
burned

with
the
Holy books

in
his
hands

in
Bedzin

200 Jews
were
locked

in
the
synagogue

and
burned
alive.

The Earth Heaving

I see an old man
who looks like a rabbi,
he has a white beard, white hair,
he carries a Torah,
he's leading this death march,
says Irene Opdyke.

I see a little girl
holding her mother's skirt
with all her might.
A beautiful woman in her
last months of pregnancy, I see.

We're just a few women, men,
standing, watching.
What can we do?
It's a long, long procession:
men hobbling on crutches,
old women,

children, all sizes, all ages,
the little ones screaming
Mama! Mama!
the big ones too scared to cry,
the eyes asking:
What did I do? What did I do?

It's a nightmare:
bodies into a shallow grave
they're plowing,
the earth heaving with the breath
of those buried alive.

Irene Opdyke, a Polish Catholic, hid 12 Jews during the German occupation of Poland. She was honored by Yad Vashem.

To Release Children

I made the effort,
and it was possible for me
to shoot only children.
It so happened that
the mothers led the children
by the hand. My neighbor
then shot the mother,
and I shot the child
that belonged to her,
because I reasoned with
myself that, after all,
without its mother
the child could not live
any longer. It was
supposed to be, so to speak,
soothing to my conscience
to release children
unable to live
without their mothers.

World Enemy

the struggle
for world domination
will be fought
entirely between us—
between Germans
and Jews.
all else is façade
and illusion—
even when we have
driven the Jews
out of Germany
he remains
our world enemy.

—*Adolf Hitler*

On the Doorstep

To the woman who will
find my daughter—
dear lady—
I leave in your care
my child, my treasure!
I beg of you,
as you are a mother yourself,
save my baby.
She doesn't need much.
She's being fed every three hours.
A buttered roll and warm milk with sugar.
Oatmeal with butter and milk.
Once a day carrot juice with sugar.
When she cries
please give her a little
light tea with sugar.
She also cries when wet.
I will try and send you the baby's clothes
as soon as possible.

Denounce a Jew

denounce a Jew
and cash in

on a sack of salt
a kilo of sugar

a Jew

for a bottle of vodka
or a pair of boots

for every Jew
you turn in

pocket fifty
franks

about a dollar
a Jew.

June 10, 1940:
The Technical Model
for a Coke-Heated Oven
to Incinerate Bodies
in Auschwitz,

is made at J.A. Topf and Sons in Erfurt,
a machine and heating technology construction business.
The model is designated D-57253.
It is commissioned by the central office
of the SS Department of Budget and Buildings
(*Haushalft und Bauten*)
for the SS Office of New Construction at Auschwitz C.C.
The oven has two combustion points
and is called a double-muffler incinerator.

No Pity

As far as the Jews are concerned,
I want to tell you quite frankly
that they must be done away with
in one way or another...
Gentlemen, I must ask you
to rid yourself
of all feeling of pity.
We must annihilate
the Jews.

---

*Hans Frank Governor, General of occupied Poland. Cabinet Session
–Krakow, Dec. 13, 1941.*

We Shot Them Still in Flight

I also took part in the day before yesterday's huge mass killing of Jews in Belorussia...when the first truckload arrived my hand was slightly trembling when shooting, but one gets used to this. When the tenth load arrived I was already aiming more calmly and shot securely at the many women, children and infants...infants were flying in a wide circle through the air and we shot them still in flight, before they fell into the pit and the water. Let's get rid of this scum that tossed all of Europe into the war.

Oct. 5, 1941 Letter to his wife from Walter Mattner, a former Viennese clerk in the Einsatzgruppen.

Waiting To Die

I simply can't believe that one day
I'll be able to leave this house
without the yellow star.
The little faith I used to have
has been completely shattered.
If God existed, he would certainly
not have permitted human beings to be
thrown alive into furnaces
and the heads of little toddlers smashed
with the butt of guns...
I saw a soldier tear a baby
only a few months old
out of a mother's hands
and bash his head
against an electric pylon.
The baby's brain splashed on the wood.
The mother went crazy.
I'm young, I'm 14,
I haven't seen much in my life.
Now I'm terrified when I see uniforms.
I'm turning into an animal
waiting to die.

---

*From the diary of Rutka Laskier. Rutka and her family were deported to Auschwitz,
where she was apparently killed on arrival.*

A Piece of Bread

the cries
of the hungry beggar children
are terribly insistent
you can hear their voices at eleven
even twelve at night—
how hard your heart
you have to
throw down a piece of bread—
in front of 24 Muranowska Street
a six-year-old boy
lay gasping all night
too weak to roll over
for the piece of bread
thrown to him
from the balcony.

Emanuel Ringleblum: Notes from the Warsaw Ghetto.

Ghetto Child

sells armbands
on Smocza Street,
does a brisk business.
squeezes through the wall,
on the Aryan side
begs a few groszy.
in his clothes
potatoes, onions, flour, sugar.
Hand hock, Jude!
gets typhus,
not allowed to work,
not allowed a ration card.
grabs food from people,
eats it on the spot.
lies naked
on Murawowska Street.
who can afford
the burial tax?

Batch After Batch—
The Great *Aktion*

From the Kovno Ghetto diary
of Avraham Tory

October 28, 1941

...the procession, numbering some 10,000 proceeding from the small ghetto
to the Ninth Fort, lasted from dawn until noon. Elderly people, and those
who were sick, collapsed by the roadside and died. Warning shots
were fired incessantly all along the way...thousands of curious Lithuanians
flocked to both sides of the road to watch the spectacle...In the fort,
the wretched people were immediately set upon by the Lithuanian killers,
who stripped them of every available article—gold rings, earrings, bracelets.
They forced them to strip naked, pushed them into pits...and fired into each pit
with machine guns...the murderers did not have time to shoot everybody
in one batch before the next batch of Jews arrived. They were accorded
the same treatment as those who had preceded them. They were pushed
into the pit on top of the dead, the dying and those still alive from the
previous group. So it continued, batch after batch, until the 10,000 men,
women and children had been butchered.

Not Much Will Remain

resettlement
of the Jews eastward—
here a fairly
barbaric process
is utilized—
of the Jews themselves
not much
will remain.

Joseph Goebbels diary entry March 27, 1942.

Excerpts from Abraham Lewin's
Diary of the Warsaw Ghetto: 1942

29 July: A Jew is seized by a bulldog taught to
                  attack only Jews with armbands.
3 August: 56 Jewish prisoners killed at the cemetery.
7 August: Today I had no bread. I ate a pickle.
9 August: All cows—120—taken away from the farm.
11 August: Aunt Chawa and Dora Fejga seized and deported—
                  they pay no attention to papers.
16 August: Women seized yesterday were freed
                  if they sacrificed their children.
22 August: Worried. Frightened.

At One Fell Swoop

RECEIVED ALARMING REPORT ABOUT PLAN BEING DISCUSSED
AND CONSIDERED IN FÜHRER HEADQUARTERS TO EXTERMINATE
AT ONE FELL SWOOP ALL JEWS IN GERMAN-CONTROLLED COUNTRIES
COMPRISING THREE AND A HALF TO FOUR MILLION
AFTER DEPORTATION AND CONCENTRATION IN THE EAST
THUS SOLVING JEWISH QUESTION ONCE AND FOR ALL   STOP
CAMPAIGN PLANNED FOR AUTUMN   STOP
METHODS BEING DISCUSSED INCLUDING HYDROCYANIC ACID
STOP

August 1942 Telegram sent to the U.S. Government and England from Gerhart Riegner, an official of the World Jewish Congress in Switzerland. This warning was met with disbelief in the State Department and no copies as requested were sent to Jewish leaders in the allied countries including Rabbi Stephen Wise in New York.

Returning from Work
We Walk Through the Gates
Into Puddles of Blood,

broken bottles, chairs, luggage strewn
all over the place,
children's bodies, heads smashed in.
We're speechless, scared, says Maja Zarch.
Our barrack is like a morgue.
Going to the toilet, we hear voices calling,
urgent, faint voices.
Are we going mad, there's no one?
Then we see two teenage boys deep in excrement,
only faces stick out.
They're on their last breath, here all day.
We run to find some men, they drag them out.
Here in Dvinsk, we huddle together tonight,
waiting for them to come for us.

Not Even
Four Years Old

August 17, 1942:
28 children
not even 4 years old
most without their parents
are deported from France
to Auschwitz
to the gas:

Micheline Perl
        aged 3
Nicole Rozenberg
        aged 3
Ginette Moszkowica
        aged 3
Rosette Frankel
        aged 3
Michelle Glowinski
        aged 3
Micheline Weinstrock
        aged 2
Helene Berger
        aged 2
Liliane Birenbaum
        aged 3
Huguette Gutmannster
        aged nearly 3
Simon Goldstein
        aged 2
Rozette Sznorman
        aged 3
Max Karpensztsrig
        aged 3
Albert Poznanski
        aged 3

Simone Gotlib
        aged nearly 3
Jacques & Francoise Brabanner
        twins, aged 3
Micheline Zaborowski
        aged 3
Sara Winter
        aged 3
Jacqueline Meichel
        aged 2
Jacqueline Gladkevizer
        aged 2
Henry Zelago
        aged 3
Marguerite Jakubovitch*
        aged 3
Jeannette Jubiler
        aged 2
Denise Kohl
        aged 3
Paul Szpanger
        aged 2
Anny Szneider
        aged 3
Victor Szbeuder
        aged 3

Marguerite Jakubovitch was deported with her six brothers and sisters; the oldest was only 10 years old.

From the Diary of Austrian Infantryman Hubert Pfoch on His Way by Train with His Company to the Eastern front. August 22, 1942

A little distance from our track we see a huge crowd. I estimate 7,000 men, women and children squatting or lying down on the ground. If they get up the guards begin shooting. We hear the rumor that these people are a Jewish transport. They call out to us they've been traveling two days without food or water. Corpses killed the night before are thrown on a lorry, it comes and goes four times. Volunteer Ukrainian SS guards, some drunk, screaming, shooting, cram 180 people into each car, parents in one, children in another—they don't care how they separate families, hitting them so viciously they break their rifle butts. *Water, my gold ring for water*, they call. Others offer us 5,000 zlotys for a cup of water. Some manage to climb out through the ventilating holes—the moment they hit the ground they're shot—a massacre that makes us sick to our souls, a blood bath such as I never dreamed of. A mother jumps down with her baby, stares calmly into the barrel of a gun—a moment later we hear the guard boast: *Did them with one shot, one shot through both heads.*

Along the Tracks

before
they left
their lives
they left
their pictures
they left
scribbled
frantic
messages
on the back
in shaky
handwriting
asking
for help.

O so many
Jewish
families—
the
smiling
faces
of the young
and old
scattered
along
the
tracks
to the
camps.

Found in a
Crumpled Torn Envelope
on the Tracks
to Auschwitz

My dears,
on the way to Poland!!!
Nothing helped.
Tried everything.
Allegedly it's going
to Metz.
Fifty of us in one car!!
Stripped of everything
in Drancy.
Be brave and courageous.
I'll be the same.
Kisses, Otto

A railway worker found this letter from Otto Simmonds to his wife—sent it to her in a new envelope with a note… "having found this letter on the rails after one of the Jews who passed through…hope this letter will reach you."

Large Shipments of Baggage
Sent to the Ghetto,

people puzzled,
bundles contain clothing, linen,

bedding, shirts, slips rolled together
three or four at a time.

pants rolled up
with a few pair of unmentionables.

jackets and coats
ripped along their seams.

no knapsacks or suitcases.

documents, letters, papers,
ID cards fall out.

often there are papers
drawn up in this ghetto.

there are many *taleysim.*

Chronicle of the Lodz ghetto, May 30–31, 1942.

From the Chronicle of the Lodz Ghetto: September 1–18, 1942

56 deaths, no births on September 1.

46 deaths, no births on September 2.

62 deaths, 2 births (1 boy, 1 girl) on September 3.

35 deaths, no births on September 4.

93 deaths, no births on September 5 and 6.

47 deaths, no births on September 7.

53 deaths, no births on September 8.

68 deaths, no births on September 9.

72 deaths, no births on September 10.

51 deaths, no births on September 11.

68 deaths, no births on September 12 and 13.

29 deaths, 1 boy born on September 14.

29 deaths, no births on September 15 and 16.

26 deaths, 2 boys, 3 girls born on September 17.

16 deaths, no births on September 18.

Lodz Ghetto: Friday, September 4, 1942

the deportation of children and old people is a fact.
children up to the age of ten are to be torn away
from their parents, brothers and sisters, and deported.
if there were the slightest assurance,
the slightest ray of hope they were being sent somewhere,
then the ghetto would not be in such a turmoil.
the ghetto is swimming in tears.
there is no house, no home, no family
which is not affected by this dreadful edict.
all hearts are icy, all hands are wrung,
all eyes filled with despair.
all faces are twisted,
all heads bowed to the ground,
all blood weeps.
tears flow by themselves.
they can't be held back.
no one can help us in any way,
no one can save us.

From the journal of Jozef Zeckowcz.

Objects of Some Kind?

storming the hospital
the SS toss naked infants
out the windows—

thinking at first
they were
objects of some kind,

Ben Edelbaum
watches in horror
as a laughing SS man

catches
a wailing infant
on his bayonet—

down the knife
blood flowing,
flowing.

Ein Reich, Ein Volk, Ein Führer

out of nowhere
into Terezín they come:
hundreds of children
fiercely guarded by the SS.

holding each other's hands
the bigger ones
help the smaller ones
struggling to keep up.

some are only four,
says Hanna Greenfield.
look, in the rain:
skeletons in rags

wet rags
to little bodies, clinging:
a column of
marching ghosts

this enemy
this Jewish enemy
this seed
that must be cut out.

Treblinka

...in a house maintained by the Germans
for the extermination of Jews,
men, women, and children comply with the order for disrobing...
urged on by whips of the Germans,
the children with women go first,
faster and faster they are driven
and thicker and thicker
fall the blows on heads paralyzed with terror and pain.
the silence of the woods is shattered by screams of women
and the oaths of Germans.
the victims now realize their doom is near.
at the entrance of the death house
the No. 1 chief himself drives them to cells, freely using a whip.
the floor of the cell is slippery.
some fall and are unable to rise
because of the pressure of those behind.
small children are flung over the heads of the women.
when the cells are filled they are closed and sealed.
steam is forced through apertures
and suffocation of the victims begins.
at first cries can be heard but these gradually subside.
after 15 minutes all is silent.
the execution is over.
when the trap is opened to let bodies drop down
they fall in a compact mass, stuck together by the heat and steam.
cold water is sprayed on them with a hose,
after which the gravediggers pile the corpses on a platform
like the carcasses of slaughtered animals.
often a gravedigger is too weak to carry two bodies as ordered,
so he ties arms or legs together and runs to the burial ground,
dragging them behind him.

From The New York Times, August 8, 1943.

An Unwritten
Page of Glory

...I am referring to
the evacuation
of the Jews,
the annihilation
of the Jewish people...
this is an unwritten
and never-to-be written
page of glory
in our history.

Heinrich Himmler, Reichsführer SS, Speaking at Poznań, Poland, October 4, 1943.

Part Two: Shot

Shot

shot in the synagogue
shot up against the wall in the headlights
      of the truck
shot in the farmyard by the dung heap
shot in the hospital, the maternity ward
shot in the city, the town, the shtetl
shot in their houses, in the streets,
      in the market square
shot in the cemetery
shot in the warehouse after machine-gun muzzles
      were pushed through holes in the walls
shot in the roundups trying to escape
shot in bed
shot in their cribs
shot in the air, the baby thrown over its
      mother's head
shot because they stole a potato
shot because they were betrayed for a kilo of sugar
shot because they weren't wearing the yellow star
shot because they *were* wearing the yellow star

shot by the *Einsatzgruppen*
shot by the Reserve Battalion of the German
       Order Police
shot by the Gestapo Firing Squad
shot by the Waffen SS and the Higher SS
shot by the Hiwis-Ukrainian, Latvian, and
       Lithuanian volunteers
shot by the Hungarian Fascist Nyilas,
       the Arrow Cross
shot by the Polish police and Polish partisans
shot by the Croatian Ustasa
shot by the Romanian army, police, gendarmerie,
       border guard, civilians, and
       the Iron Guard
shot by the *Wehrmacht*
shot by old men in the German Home Guard
shot by young boys in the Hitler Youth
shot in *Aktion* after *Aktion* as if it was
       "more or less our daily bread"
shot in the search-and-destroy mission, the
       Jew Hunt
shot in the "harvest festival," the *Erntefest*
shot in order to make the northern Lublin district
       judenrein

shot in Zhitomir, Poniatowa, Józefów, Trawniki
shot in Lomazy, Parczew, Bialystok, Kharkov
shot in Bialowieza, Luków, Riga, Poltava
shot in Międzyrzec, Khorol, Kremenstshug
shot in Slutsk, Bobruisk, Mogilev, Vinnitsa
shot in Odessa, Lvov, Kolmyja, Minsk, Rovno
shot in Majdanek and Brest-Litovsk
shot in Neu Sandau and Tarnopol and Rohatin
shot in Dnepropetrovsk
shot in Kovno, Pinsk, Berdichev, Tarnów
shot in Kamenets-Podolski
shot in Krakow, Szczebrzeszyn, Siauliai
shot in Stolin, Kielce, Lutsk, Serokomla
shot in Drogobych, Luga, Delatyn
shot in the Warsaw Ghetto
shot in the ravine of Babi Yar
shot in Bilgoraj, Nadvornaya, Stanislawów
shot in David Grodek, Janów Podlesia
shot near Zamosc

shot after nobody thought they would be shot because
        they were told "get ready, the entire Jewish
        population is going to spend the winter on a farm"
shot after being roped with their families, roped
        with barbed wire
shot after being told they would be spared if they
        came out of hiding and reported for a new
        identity card
shot while hiding up to their necks in excrement
        in the public outhouse
shot after being tied together in threes—only the
        middle person shot, his weight pulling down
        the other two, after being shoved in the river
shot marching to the shooting site because they
        lagged behind
shot after the Star of David was branded on their foreheads
shot lying face down, naked, waiting for hours
        in the hot August sun
shot after being paraded through the streets—the
        women, naked, arms in the air, marching through
        the snow and ice to the forest

shot walking across a plank laid over the grave
shot after being driven into the grave and made to
      lie down on top of those who had been
      shot before them
shot after their eyes were gouged out because they
      refused to undress
shot in the neck, their heads stuck in a pot
shot in the mouth after being forced to crawl through
      a mud hole, singing
shot in the back of the head, brains splattering
      on the green uniforms
shot one after another, forcing the rabbi to watch,
      saving him for last
shot while the shooter ate an apple

shot because they were too weak to walk to the gas van
shot because they didn't take off their hats
       to the guards
shot when they sat down, after the guard told them:
       "Take it easy. Rest a while."
shot marching to the *Umschlagplatz* because they walked
       too fast, because they fell, because they strayed
       out of line, because they turned their heads,
       because they bent down, because they spoke too loud,
       because they were children who cried
shot after being placed in a row for target practice,
       bottles on their heads
shot after being raped—"going to peel potatoes,"
       the Germans called it
shot after benches were placed at the shooting site
       so local Lithuanians could get a good view
shot after uttering the first words of the Kaddish:
       Yitgodal veyitkadach shmé...

shot in the courtyard of Block 11 at Auschwitz, at
  the "Death Wall," after their breasts were singed,
  their fingernails extracted
shot because the baby was alive at its mother's breast
  after the doors of the gas chamber opened
shot because they couldn't walk a straight line
shot trying to scoop some soup from the bottom of the
  empty pot
shot in the "hat trick"—the guard threw the prisoner's
  hat in the air, ordered him to run after it, then
  shot him trying to escape
shot after dismantling the camp
shot in the moments before liberation, the surrender
  leaflets dropping into the camp, the commander
  yelling: "We may have only two minutes to live,
  but you have only one."

Poster, Belzec Platform

First a wash
and breakfast—
then to work.

Death *Kommando*

In Belzec
able-bodied Jews
were selected
from the transports
for the
Death *Kommando*.

they dug the graves
dragged bodies
out of the death chamber
piled them
in a huge mound
then dumped them
into their graves.

Rudolf Reder
one of only two
Belzec survivors
recalls how
the corpses' heads
dug in the sand
as he dragged them.

he carried
the bodies of children
two at a time
one over
each shoulder.

he covered the bodies
with a huge
layer of sand
while thick black blood
flowed out
flooding the graves
like a lake.

Hidden

Almost nine out of ten Jewish children
who were alive before World War II
died during the Holocaust.

——Debórah Dwork

Hidden because you look Jewish and can't pass as Aryan.
Hidden as a Catholic child.
Hidden as an orphan from a bombed out city.
Hidden because you're a girl, and girls can be saved easier
          than boys.
Hidden disguised as a girl.
Hidden with false documents.
Hidden young with no concept or memory of Jewish life.
Hidden on the Aryan side after being smuggled out of the ghetto.
Hidden in the ghetto before being kidnapped by the Jewish police
          and deported to Auschwitz.
Hidden in an attic, a closet, a dark flea-infested cellar.
Hidden between walls.
Hidden in a stove.
Hidden night after night in a cold, dark, open grave in the
          Jewish cemetery, without your doll, without your mother,
          while the Nazis rounded up the children in the ghetto.
Hidden starving in a wardrobe for two and a half years.
Hidden underneath the floorboards of the barn.
Hidden in a garden shed, a chicken coop, a forest hut,
          a cave, a bunker.
Hidden in a 4x6 hole covered with a plank of wood,
          your only occupation killing lice.
Hidden in an orphanage, a convent, a boarding school,
          a tiny village in the mountains.
Hidden in a straw loft in a pigsty.
Hidden in a dug-out space under the pigsty,
          the pig urine seeping down on you.
Hidden in a little house where the dog used to sleep.
Hidden in the straw-covered floor of a pigeon coop,
          pigeon droppings landing on you day and night.

Hidden in a sewer in a summer dress, shaking from the cold,
     smelly water seeping in, red rats big as chickens,
     yellow worms crawling all over.
Hidden into silence—you can't cry, you can't laugh.
Hidden until a collaborator informs on you—your foster family
     shot as a warning in front of the neighbors.
Hidden in a knapsack on a father's back until the bayonet
     turns it into a bloody soaked rag.

Judenjagd
Jew Hunt

We were told there were many Jews hiding in the forest.
We searched through the woods in a skirmish line
but could find nothing. The Jews were obviously well hidden.
We combed the woods a second time.
Only then could we discover individual chimney pipes
sticking out of the earth.
Jews had hidden themselves in underground bunkers.
They were hauled out with resistance in only one bunker.
Some of our comrades climbed down into this bunker
and hauled the Jews out.
The Jews were then shot on the spot...the Jews had to lie
face down on the ground and were killed by a neck shot...
the men standing nearby were ordered to shoot them.
Some fifty Jews were shot, including men and women of all ages,
because entire families had hidden themselves there...
the shooting took place quite publicly...
a number of Poles from Parczew were standing
directly by the shooting site.
They were then ordered to bury the Jews
who had been shot in a half-finished bunker.

Testimony from Third Company; Reserve Police Battalion 101; Office of the State Prosecutor; Hamburg 1957/62.

Pictures Were *Verboten,*

but on the day of the massacre of the Jews
in Liepaja, some *Einsatzgruppen* officer
eager for a souvenir
orders four women and a young girl
to face his camera.

Five abreast (they went to the pits in fives),
arms locked, they stand close-pressed.
In the snow, barefoot, shivering
in their underwear, they stand.
Women were allowed to keep their shifts.

Eyes narrowed, mouths compressed,
they squeeze hands, stare into the lens
(one woman closes her eyes).
The older woman, the grandmother, grimacing,
is flanked by her three daughters.
Her nine-year-old granddaughter, still
in her bonnet, bows her head, hiding
behind her mother on the end.
One of the women in her twenties, pretty,
cocks her head, raises a hand,
as if to preen her long black hair.

In the background, blurred heaps of
clothing, shoes, rucksacks, people undressing,
soldiers in long overcoats, rifles
on their shoulders. In the women's ears,
the burst of machine guns, screams,
the shouted prayers of those groups of five
going before them.

Brains, Blood, and Bone Splinters

before the shootings in Józefów
the men stood around in a semicircle

the battalion doctor
sketched on the ground

the outline of the upper part
of a man's body

marking on the neck
the spot at which they should fire

at first they aimed too high
the entire skull exploded

brains blood & bone splinters
sprayed everywhere

often the entire skull
or rear skullcap

was torn off.

Sardinenpackung

The *Einsatzgruppen*
were frustrated.
Jews shot at the edge
of the open pits
were falling
on top of those
shot before them.
Bodies crumpled
every which way.
This made for unused,
wasted space.
What to do?
SS and police general
Friedrich Jeckeln
solved the problem.
Before they were
shot in the neck,
Jews had to lie
face down on those
shot before them.
Layer upon layer.
The Germans called this
Sardinenpackung—
sardine-packing.

In the Pit

In the pit Rita Weiss sees her companions:
some still move, convulsively:

a rifle volley, loud, silence, dark.
is this death?

I try to raise my arm, but can't.
I open my eyes, nothing.

I sit up, fresh branches
brush my head.

dark, no stars, my mind clears,
I cry out:

are any of you alive?
come out if you are.

in the pit
no one moves.

In Hiding

Our Father who art in heaven—mustn't forget
      the Lord's Prayer, the Hail Mary,
      mustn't forget to make the sign of the cross,
      mustn't forget I can't pee in front of other boys.
But—*If I forget you, O Jerusalem*—how will
      my parents find me when they come back?
And everybody comes back.
And they light the *Shabbat* candles.
And I, who can't remember my name, can't remember
      who I was, I am not there.

Jedwabne

*Based on the deposition of Szmul Wasersztajn, the first at war's end to
condemn his Polish neighbors rather than the Germans, for the massacre of
nearly the entire population of sixteen hundred Jews from the Polish village
of Jedwabne.*

With mine own eyes I see our local Polish
kill Chajcia Wasersztajn, fifty-three, Jakub Kac, seventy-three,
and Eliasz Krawiecki.
With bricks they stone to death Jakub Kac.
Krawiecki they knife,
then pluck his eyes and cut off his tongue.
He suffers terribly for twelve hours
before giving up his soul.
Wacek Borowski with his brother Mietk
I see them with others walking from one Jewish dwelling to another,
they are playing accordion and flute
to drown the screams of our Jewish women and children.
The local Polish hooligans,
armed with axes, clubs studded with nails,
and other instruments of torture,
chase the Jews into the street where they are
clubbed and hacked to death.
Jews are ordered to dig a hole and bury all
previously murdered Jews,
then those are killed and in turn buried by others.
The beards of old Jews are burned,
newborn babies are killed at their mothers' breasts,
people are beaten and forced to sing and dance,
the Jews are ordered to line up in a column four in a row;
in front, they put the ninety-year-old rabbi
and the *shochet* (Kosher butcher),
a red banner they give them—
and all are ordered to sing as they're beastly beaten
and chased into the barn.
Various instruments they are playing in order to drown out
the screams of the victims.
Some Jews try to defend themselves, but they're defenseless.
Bloodied and wounded, they're pushed into the barn.

The barn's doused with kerosene and lit.
Then the local Polish go around to search Jewish homes
to look for the remaining sick and children.
The sick they carry to the barn,
the little children they rope together by their legs,
carry them on their back,
put them on pitchforks and throw them into
the smoldering coals.

---

10 July 2002: on national TV from Jedwabne, Poland, President Aleksander Kwasniewski asks forgiveness for this "particularly cruel crime." A sign on several doors in the village reads: "We do not apologize."

Judeocide Bookkeeping

listing their achievements
Einsatzgruppen & German Police

send regular dispatches
to Berlin—

SS *Standartenführer* Karl Jager
reports from Lithuania:

16 August: killed 3,200 Jews,
Jewesses & Jewish children.

23 August: killed 1,312 Jews,
612 Jewesses & 1,609 Jewish children.

1 December: to date killed
33,346 Jews

our objective to solve
the Jewish problem for Lithuania

has been solved.

From the Diary of SS Sergeant Felix Landau, A Member of *Einsatzkommando* in Drohobyez

We go into the wood and look for a spot suitable for mass executions.
We order the prisoners to dig their graves. Only two of them are crying,
the others show courage. What can they all be thinking? I believe each
still has the hope of not being shot. I don't feel the slightest stir of pity.
Slowly the grave gets bigger and deeper. Two are crying without let-up.
I let them dig more so they can think. The work really calms them.
Money, watches, and valuables are collected. The two women go first
to be shot; placed at the edge of the grave they face the soldiers.
They get shot. When it's the men's turn, the soldiers aim at the shoulder.
All our six men are allowed to shoot. Three prisoners have been shot
in the heart. The shooting goes on. Two heads have been shot off. Nearly
all fall into the grave unconscious only to suffer a long while. Our
revolvers don't help either. The last group have to throw the corpses
into the graves—they have to stand ready for their own execution.
They all tumble into the grave.

Part Three: The Final Solution

The Führer Has Ordered the Final Solution of the Jewish Question,

and we the SS are to carry out this order.
The extermination centers already existing in the east
are not in a position to carry out the operation
on the large scale planned.
I have therefore selected Auschwitz for this purpose:
it is situated conveniently from the
point of view of transportation,
and it will be easy to seal off and camouflage.
You will keep this order absolutely confidential,
even from your superiors.
After you talk with Eichmann, you should
immediately send me the plans for the projected
installations. The Jews are age-old enemies
of the German people and must be eliminated.
All Jews whom we can lay hands on during the war
will be put to death without exception.

Heinrich Himmler as reported in the autobiography of Rudolf Hoess.

The Final Solution

I am *Endlösung*
The Final Solution to the Jewish problem.
I was nurtured on centuries
of hate and vitriol.
I now reside in a genocidal state
called Nazi Germany.

I target every Jew in Europe—
see how my death squads
round up the Jews
in village after village.
I am oblivious to their wailing
pleas and cries.

I shoot Jews into the pits,
grab babies out of their mother's arms,
swing them by their legs,
bash their heads against the wall.

I lock men, women & children
into barns & set them on fire.
I hang Jews. Drown Jews.
Beat & work & starve Jews to death.

I throw Jews down the stone quarries.
I shove Jews to death over the cliffs.
I stuff Jews into the death trains.
I gas Jews with my *Zyklon B*.

I have no pity, no remorse.
Jews are not pure Aryan.
Jews are subhuman vermin.
Jews are the enemy
and must be eliminated.

I am The Final Solution.
Look for me in the ashes.

**Chalk Marks Observed by
Polish Railwayman Franciszek Zabecki
on the Side of a Train on the Treblinka Platform
the Morning of July 23, 1942**

~~120~~

~~150~~

~~180~~

200

Take a Deep Breath

nothing at all
is going to happen to you

you must take a deep breath
in the chambers

that expands
the lungs

the inhalation
is necessary

because of illnesses
and infection.

Instructions given to Jews entering the gas chambers at Belzec—as reported by SS officer Kurt Gerstein.

Whatever You Can Carry

*Twenty-nine storerooms were burned before the liberation of Auschwitz.
In the six that remained they discovered 348,820 men's suits, 836,255
women's coats, more than seven tons of human hair and even 13,964
carpets.*

              –Michael Berenbaum: *The World Must Know*

"You will work in the factory, work in
the fields, you will be resettled in the East,
bring whatever you can carry."

So our dresses, shirts, suits, underwear,
bedsheets, featherbeds, pillows, tablecloths,
towels, we carried.

We carried our hairbrushes, handbrushes,
toothbrushes, shoe daubers, scissors, mirrors,
safety razors. Forks, spoons, knives,

pots, saucepans, tea strainers, potato
peelers, can openers we carried. We carried
umbrellas, sunglasses, soap, toothpaste,

shoe polish. We carried our photographs.
We carried milk powder, talc,
baby food.

We carried our sewing machines. We carried
rugs, medical instruments,
the baby's pram.

Jewelry we carried,
sewn in our shoes, sewn in our corsets,
hidden in our bodies.

We carried loaves of bread, bottles of wine,
schnapps, cocoa, chocolate, jars of marmalade,
cans of fish. Wigs, prayer shawls,

tiny Torahs, skullcaps, phylacteries we carried.
Warm winter coats in the heat of summer
we carried. On our coats, our suits,

our dresses, we carried our yellow stars.
On our baggage in bold letters, our addresses,
our names we carried.

We carried our lives.

To Auschwitz, Standing

Before they seal the doors
the Gestapo is putting
two buckets in each wagon:
one with drinking water,
the other empty for excrement,
says Irme Reiner.
at train stops we are crying out,
but they're never filled,
never emptied.
our children, our sick,
our old, can't take the heat,
the lack of air,
the foul smell, no room to sit—
so they're dying,
along with those who slashed
their wrists—
but the Gestapo
won't let us take them out
and bury them—
they travel with us
to Auschwitz, standing.

The Doors Are Torn Open

Alle heraus!

Everybody out!

Out, out! Los, los! Schneller!

Where are we?

Who could be cooking meat
at this hour?

Good morning, Fräulein.

My umbrella?

Verboten.

Moshe, go find out why I should
give up the baby to an older woman?

My wedding ring? My watch?

Verboten, verboten.

Water, water! Of course, of course.

Sir, what's going to happen
to us?

Mamele! I want to go with you.

Men left. Women right.

Sara, where are you?

Luggage afterwards. Together

afterwards.

Give It to Your Mother

on the platform
in Auschwitz they stood—

young women holding babies
in their arms—

watching while other
young women with babies

are waved to the side
with the old ones—

in their ear
someone is whispering

give it to your mother
give it to your mother-in-law

don't be a fool you can
save your life—

some of them did—
they handed their babies

to the older women
while they went

to the working side
with the younger women—

their babies went
to the gas.

Red Flames
and Ashes

as we marched
from off the train
we could see chimneys
spewing
these red flames
up into the sky,
said Halina Laster.
ashes fell
over everything—
grey ashes—
they came
on your fingers
like silk.
and we just said:
my God, these are
human ashes.

The Killing Centers

trains
every day they're coming
three times daily
fifty cars each
sometimes more
                        —Belzec

the merchandise aboard the sealed vans
displays a tendency to rush to the rear doors
and is mainly found lying there
at the end of the operation
                        —Chełmno

seven gas chambers
three wooden gallows
                        —Majdanek

death in the morning
death in the afternoon
death at night
                        —Auschwitz

fewer than a hundred survivors
                        —Treblinka

fifty survivors
                        —Sobibor

In the Fire

Arriving in Auschwitz
around one o'clock in the morning,
Alexander Ehrmann remembers
floodlights, tall chimney, stench, flames,
dogs barking,
commands he didn't understand:
Schnell, Raus, raus, raus!
strange uniformed men in striped clothes
telling us to get in formations of five
and leave all the luggage.
I ask one of the guys:
tell me where we're going?
he points towards the flames.
we walk down an alley—
piles of rubble, branches—
the sentries screaming *lauf lauf*—
a baby I hear crying,
but I can't stop and look—
it smells a horrible stench,
and I knew that things in the fire
were moving,
there were babies
in the fire.

Jude Juif Jood J

we are flowing like a ragged yellow river out of the boxcars
raus raus raus the whips cracking the dogs the flames
shooting stench of burning meat *water water*
what is happening to us as we surge past the rows of barbed wire
throwing our bread our watches over the fence to the
striped skeletons those other yellow stars who will gather us
from heaping piles from numbered pegs in the undressing room.

Those That Went Left

we
  walk
    dazed
    walk
      thirsty
        not
          knowing
          which
          is
          the
          good
          side
          later
            in
            the
              lager
              we
                find
                  out
                    right
                    is
                    the
                    good
                    side
                    those
                    that
                      went
                        left
                    we
                    never
                    see
                  again.

Auschwitz

death death death death death death death death death death death
death death death death death death death death death death death
death death death death death death death death death death death
death death death death death death death death death death death
death death death death death death death death death death death
death death death death death death death death death death death
death death death death death death death death death death death
death death death death death death death death death death death
death death death death death death death death death death death
death death death death death death death death death death death
death death death death death death death death death death death
death death death death death death death death death death death
death death death death death death death death death death death
death death death death death death death death death death death
death death death death death death death death death death death
death death death death death death death death death death death
death death death death death death death death death death death
death death death death death death death death death death death
death death death death death death death death death death death
death death death death death death death death death death death
death death death death death death death death death death death
death death death death death death death death death death death
death death death death death death death death death death death
death death death death death death death death death death death
death death death death death death death death death death death
death death death death death death death death death death death
death death death death death death death death death death death
death death death death death death death death death death death
death death death death death death death death death death death
death death death death death death death death death death death
death death death death death death death death death death death
death death death death death death death death death death death

I Don't Want a Number,

if I get a number,
I be a gonner:
but they appear
on my arm
my left forearm:
tattoo of blue numbers.
I am *Häftling*
I am ordinary prisoner
I am *87492*
my number is my name
I have been baptised.

No Why

in Auschwitz
Primo Levi

driven
by thirst

reaches outside
his barrack

breaks off
an icicle—

a guard
grabs it—

Why?
asks Levi—

*hier ist
kein warum*

here
says the guard

*there is
no why.*

In the Dutch Deportation Center of Westerbork on the Eve of Deportation to Auschwitz

You would think it's just another
picture of a bunch of kids,

ten- or eleven-year-old kids
gathered together for some final

instructions before setting out
on their class picnic.

You see the star with its Dutch word
for Jew, *Jood*, marking the left front

of jackets and dresses. Marking
twin girls in the third row.

One looks away, the other puckers up
her lips, stares into the lens.

Some boys wear ties. Most girls
wear checkered dresses. Hair ribbons

blossom: wild white flowers among
dark somber faces, blank quizzical

faces, eyes looking for answers.
You notice a single adult,

a middle-aged man in a suit
and tie. What did he know?

Did he sit with other children
in other pictures? Would he go

to the wagons tomorrow morning with
the children? Where are the SS?

And then it hits you that this
Westerbork is the same place where

Anne Frank and her family would
leave in the last transport

for Auschwitz, leave only months
after the children in this picture

were deported. Was there a similar
picture somewhere of Anne Frank?

Look: in the back row, that chubby
boy in the sailor suit is pulling

his mouth apart, hamming it up:
a class clown just like you were

back in 1944, the year this picture
was taken, the year you graduated

from Ravinia Grammar School,
the year you remember thinking

Hitler and Goering were some kind of
comedy act, like Abbott and Costello.

Twins

Mengele hoped to produce a master race of
blond, blue-eyed Aryans. Twins were the key.
—Sheila Cohn Dekel

As they got off the cattle car
the guards called for twins.
Torn from their mother's skirt,
they were taken to Barrack 31 in Auschwitz.
(Some mothers hid their twins' identity,
they went directly to the gas.)

Twins kept their hair, clothes, names.
They had no number, no tattoo, no stripes.
If they stole a potato, a slice of bread,
even the most brutal camp guards wouldn't
beat them because they were Mengele's twins.
They belonged to Uncle Mengele.

Picked up every morning by fake Red Cross
trucks, the twins were taken to Mengele's labs.
Blood was taken from fingers, necks, arms,
sometimes both arms at the same time.
Some fainted. Some were rewarded with a
sugar cube from Mengele.

Naked, twins were marked, painted, measured,
observed. Needles and chemicals were
stuck in eyes, pins in heads. They were
forced to live in straw-strewn cages. Infected
with typhus, tuberculosis. Spines were operated
on, again and again.

Boys were castrated, girls sterilized. They
tried to make girls out of boys and boys
out of girls. Without anesthesia, twins were
sewed together, their veins were sewed.
Arms and legs cut off. Pieces of stomachs,
hearts, and sex organs sent to Berlin
stamped *War Material—Urgent.*

120

Am I Still a Human Being?

cold   bewildered
clothes taken   shoes taken
head shaved   body shaved
arm tattooed   my name is my number
no underwear   wooden shoes
striped clothing
I'm going   to die anyway
thought Maria Salinger
so I turned   went straight to
the electric fence
some people   ran after me
schlepped me back.

Remember Your Number

outside were signs
Baths and *Sauna*

then they were brought to the
Entkleidungskammer (dressing room)

there were benches
and clothes hooks with numbers

they had to undress
and the SS man told them

remember your
clothes hook number

Testimony of Yehuda Bakon from the trial of Adolf Eichmann.

Es Geht Mir Gut

In the undressing room
in Birkenau

Jews were given postcards
to write home.

Each had to say:
Es geht mir gut.

I am well.

Stone

you search for your mother
spotting your old rebbe

turning pink with green spots
pink with red spots

pink from the gas

pink the flowers
you remember in the garden

before you walk down the steps
to the disinfection

before you hang your clothes
on the hook

walking with the others
naked

before you find out
the piece of soap is

stone.

Zyklon B

Looked like starch, grainy,
bluish-white, in one-pound cans,
a skull and bones on the label.

A pesticide, odorless gas,
prussic acid, made by The Degesch
Company of Frankfurt, supplied by
Tesch and Stabenon of Hamburg.

Hoess, commandant of Auschwitz,
thought it would spare his men
a great psychological burden
(versus shooting).

Saturday, March 13, 1943,
2,000 Jewish men women and children
arrive in Auschwitz from Krakow.

Following selection, 1,492 people
are taken to the baths in the new
crematorium. Within five minutes
all 1,492 are dead. It takes
two days to burn the *pieces.*

In 1945, hair found in Auschwitz
was shown to contain compounds
of prussic acid. Traces were also
discovered in hairpins, clasps,
and gold-framed glasses.

Sonderkommando

I am a Jew who drives other Jews,
       even the children, into the showers.
I untangle the bodies, drag bodies, stack bodies.
I take off spectacles, artificial legs,
       yank gold teeth from jaws.
I shear the skulls of the female corpses.
I search bodies for hidden valuables.
I collect the fat, pour it back on the flesh
       to stoke the fire.
I lubricate the corpse stretchers with soap.
I pound the skulls, crush the bones, dump the ashes
       into the pond.
I live inside the crematorium, the gas chamber.
I bury my diary, I scatter teeth, I leave a trace.

When the Screaming Stopped

we knew
they were
dead

when
the screaming
stopped.

Commandant Rudolf Hoess on the gassing at Auschwitz.

We Open
the Gas Chamber
Doors,

people fall out
like blocks of stone
says Filip Müller.
they're battered,
covered in excrement,
covered in blood.
in the dark they fought
to climb higher
where the air was:
a death struggle.
the strongest
end up on top.
the old, the weak,
the children
with crushed skulls,
on the bottom.

Among the Heap

among
the
heap

of
gassed
bodies

a
baby
sucking

still
sucking
on

its
mother's
breast—

thrown
alive
into

the
flames.

In the Oven

in the oven
we put outside
the women:
inside
the men we shove:
fat on women
who have more than men
can burn more easily
that way.

Testimony of Sonderkommando, Darrio Gabbri.

Get Out of Here
Go Stir the Bodies

what did he mean,
"stir the bodies"?
I enter the cremation chamber,
says Filip Müller.
There's a Jewish prisoner, Fischel,
I watch him poke the fire
with a long rod.
"Do as I'm doing,
or the SS will kill you."
I pick up a steel poker,
do as he was doing.

Gold Ashes

after
the gas
gold teeth
& dentures
from the dead
they took—
after
cremation
they sifted
the ashes
to recover
any melted gold
they may have
missed.

Part Four: The Dead & Dying

Standing with the Dead

every day before dawn in the *lager*
we stand in line for the *Appell*
for hours we stand waiting to be counted
in rain or shine frost or snow we stand
the sick we drag from their bunks
the dead we prop up next to us—
the dogs are snarling
the *kapo* is clubbing us
the dead feel no pain
standing beside us
to be counted
for the last
time.

The Shooting Never Stops

shot after the synagogue was burned, the cemetery destroyed,
     the Jewish property looted
shot after Jews attacked the Ukrainian guards with knives,
     razors, and wooden clubs torn from a fence
shot after being forced in chains to dig up and burn victims
     of the Babi Yar massacre
shot in their houses, in the streets, in the market square—
     the air filled with screams and gunfire,
     the elderly, the sick, the infants left lying
     in houses, doorways and streets
shot after being taken from the ghetto to a pit on the outskirts
     of town—the children thrown into the pit alive
shot after running up to her father to say goodbye—
     ordered to open her mouth for impudence, the German
     fired a bullet into it
shot after escaping from the pit
shot while a German band was playing

shot and buried half alive because the executioners
      complained of being very tired of their work
      and having aching shoulders from shooting
shot—gunned down on the doorstep because they didn't
      leave quickly enough
shot after dragging the grandmother into the courtyard
      and shooting her in front of the whole family
shot after the crying child is seized from its mother's arms
      and shot in front of her
shot in the Jewish hospital, the wailing infants thrown
      out the windows
shot because the elderly couple made their way up the street
      dressed in their best *Shabbath* clothes
shot if they limped, if they had one leg, if a foot
      was bandaged
shot while standing naked, the women carrying babies
      sucking at their breasts

shot after breaking the small windows of the cattle car
        and jumping out—the tracks covered with corpses
shot in big batches by eighty executioners—all drunk
shot with dumdum bullets that split when they hit the body
shot—the chief executioner singing along with his
        fellow executioners
shot, but a boy escapes the pit—naked, covered with blood,
        he knocks on a peasant's door—
        Jew, go back to the grave where you belong!
shot outside Warsaw in groups for seven continuous days,
        the Jewish victims included industrialists, engineers,
        furriers, businessmen, lawyers, hatters, doctors,
        dentists, teachers, photographers, tie-makers,
        bookkeepers, chemists and musicians
shot while leaping naked into the deep graves in the
        Jewish cemetery—the Jews falling on one another
        whether dead or alive

shot in the back because he couldn't move quickly enough
        out of the ghetto—his last words:
        Schreibt und farschreibt! Write & record!
shot while each morning a group of Jews was ordered
        to watch the killings
shot after hiding without a work pass
shot after being thrown into an anti-tank ditch
        bound to one another's arms in groups
        of forty or fifty
shot after being kept for three days in underground cellars
        with ice-covered walls and no food or drink
shot in the Warsaw ghetto by the Polish police who wept
        after firing
shot in a funeral procession in the ghetto
shot down as they held hands dancing in their prayer shawls,
        shouting *lekhaim* (to life). The Germans, so enraged,
        slit their bellies and trampled on the Jews
        until their bowels came out.

shot the entire Jewish council because they refused
        to draw up a list of all old and sick Jews
        and deliver them to the Gestapo
shot because the SS man didn't like the look on
        a prisoner's face
shot after being driven unto the ice on the river—after
        firing on the ice to break it up, all those who
        managed to stay afloat were shot
shot two Jewish women because bread and cakes
        were found on them
shot in groups of five—as each group tumbled into the pit
        the commander shook the hands of the firing squad
shot fully dressed—the yellow star on the front and back
        of their coats buried with their belongings
shot after being brutally whipped to unconsciousness
        because they didn't unload the corpses fast enough
        from the gas vans
shot after unloading the corpses from the gas van
        and told to lie face down on top of the corpses
        in the ditch before being machine-gunned
        in their heads

shot after being thrown out of a window sitting in a chair
shot in the ghetto after trying to join those who were
        not to be deported
shot while their last moments were recorded
        by a German firing squad
shot shot shot shot shot shot—the shots echoing
        all over the Krakow ghetto
shot—a small baby crying, wrapped in a pillow,
        thrown out of the gas van, machine-gunned and
        tossed in the ditch—the SS men
        laughing, laughing
shot as they tried to resist boarding the death trains
shot—all those who begged for water and all those
        who tried to give it to the Jews on a train
        stopped at a station
shot after being vigorously clubbed and forced to crawl
        naked on the ground before the grave

shot through the back of the head in the ghetto after
      being told to walk straight ahead
shot to terrorize the populace in wild daily shootings
      in the streets of the Warsaw ghetto
shot after wailing and refusing to leave her husband's side
      after he was shot
shot with a whole trainload of deportees after attacking
      a Ukrainian guard because the guard refused to let him
      say farewell to his mother
shot after throwing three- and four-year-old children
      into the air in the Janowska camp
shot in Majdanek—the SS making "sport" of machine-gunning
      children in front of their parents
shot in the face at close range by a drunk SS man
shot after being made to get into the pit with buckets
      on their heads
shot by Soviet partisans after fleeing to the forest
      and refusing to give up his pistol
shot after their heads and arms were broken
shot for refusing to dig up the burial pits near the camp
      in Auschwitz

shot by trained Lithuanians after the SS called Kovno
      "a shooting paradise"
shot on the tip of the nose or a finger
      from the camp windows
shot with a bullet in the back during the death march
      because they lagged behind, because they couldn't
      walk any further, because they couldn't
      get to their feet at the start of the daily march,
      because they tried to run away,
      because they tried to help a fellow prisoner
shot on the last days of the death march after beginning
      to dance and shouting: "I have outlived Hitler,
      what more do I want?"
shot in the camp on the eve of the American arrival
shot by Poles after surviving the camps and returning
      to their former Polish towns.

Roughly as many Jews were killed by bullets as gas in the Holocaust, a fact not widely known to this day.
           —David Denby

Auschwitz, February 8, 1943

two thousand
men, women and children

arrive in transport
from Bialystok ghetto:

after selection
1,830 deportees

killed
in gas chambers.

SS notes recorded by Daunta Czech.

Judenrein

June 16,
1943—

Berlin
is
declared

Judenrein—

Clean
of
Jews.

Between 1941 & 1943 more than 60,000 Berlin Jews were deported to the camps—
almost all of those deported were killed.

Four Million Jews Waiting For Death

FOUR MILLION JEWS waiting for death.
Oh hang and burn but—quiet Jews!
Don't be bothersome; save your breath—

The world is busy with other news.

✡

Time Races Death:

What Are We Waiting For?

✡

HOW WELL ARE YOU SLEEPING?

Is There Something You Could Have Done
to Save Millions of Innocent People—
Men, Women, and Children—
from Torture And Death?

From the Bergson Group's 1943–44 Ad Campaign in The New York Times

Lice Can Kill

like the rats & bedbugs
      lice were everywhere

in the *Häftlinge*'s hair
      on their bodies, in their clothes

with no soap & little water
      how could one wash?

everyone was infested

all night they scratched
      at the bites

the bites turning into
      typhus

in *die Zentrale Sauna*
      for new arrivals

one of the signs said
      Lice Can Kill

and they did.

Death by Excrement

night & day
urine & waste
mixed with blood & pus
pour down our bunks
pour down our legs—
sometimes
it's frozen
to our legs—
smell of diarrhea
smell of corpses
mingle with
stink
from the
cremo.

Spade Handle Death

killing
Jews
in
Auschwitz
was
easy—
they
just
put
the
spade
handle
onto
the
prisoner's
neck—
dangle
his
legs
until
he
suffocates.

William Brasse, the camp photographer of prisoner photographs, said he saw this several times—Brasse managed to preserve thousands of prisoner's pictures despite an order to burn them.

Eighty Numbers

We don't know their names.
All we're left with is eighty numbers.
We know they're boys. We know
there is a Roll Call Leader called Politzch.
He leads these eighty numbers from Birkenau
to the main camp at Auschwitz.

We don't know the boys' names.
All we know is they are 13 to 17
and Polish Jews who came in the cattle cars
with their families.

Do the boys believe
they'll be taking a nursing course
as they march to the infirmary
in Block 20 on this day,
this first day of March in 1943?

Are they orphans?
Have their mothers and fathers been shot?
Gassed? How long have they been in Auschwitz?
Is the black smoke from the crematorium
thick this day? Do they smell
the burning fat and bone and hair?

We don't know their names,
but we know an SS Corporal called Sherpe
injected the boys
with lethal does of phenol
in the evening.

We don't know their names,
we do know the Germans called bodies *pieces:*
eighty *pieces* for the fire,
eighty numbers recorded by the SS:

29502	30559	32924	37112	44114
47831	57296	60308	60460	73614
73963	78174	79662	80451	82074
82192	82357	82613	82633	82747
82763	82764	82767	82782	82783
84960	86415	87924	88138	88217
90044	90062	91059	93446	93941
95086	95095	95099	95267	95272
95338	95424	95909	96159	96198
96661	96720	97242	97301	97830
98079	98525	98529	98562	98590
99278	99429	99639	99711	100184
100211	100220	100268	100309	100330
100368	100573	100642	101189	101368
101527	102485	102535	102566	102567
102691	102845	103419	103462	103504

The *Stehbunker*

stand up punishment
& suffocation cells
about 3 feet square
in the basement
of Block 11.

up to five *Häftlinge*
crammed in
at a time—
they could only
stand or crouch.

no food no water
no light—
the only bit of air
filtered through
the crack in the door.

punishment
in the
Stehbunker
could last for
ten days—

that is
if they could last—
one *Häftling*
was so hungry
he ate his shoes.

Do You See This Green Triangle?
It Means I'm a Killer

a killer *kapo*—
we called them *Grüne Spitzen*—

you were stuck with him

stuck in a bad work detail
a death detail—

any day you could be
a gonner

& every day your *Grüne Spitzen*
will show the guards

how he beats & beats you—

will your *Grüne Spitzen*
throw your soup in the mud?

will he piss on you?

will he order you to
crawl jump run

until you faint?

will your *Grüne Spitzen*
beat you to death

today or tomorrow?

The Green Triangles were recruited from violent criminal gangs and common criminals—they were known for their brutality.

Death by Beating

Vicious beatings in Mauthausen were commonplace.
Pat O'Leary, a British prisoner, remembers
watching a brutal beating in the camp.
It started with a tremendous blow
to a prisoner's jaw, followed by the SS guard
kicking a man in his stomach.
As he doubled up, blows hit his jaw,
his stomach—eight, nine, ten, eleven times,
followed by a tremendous kick
to the pit of his stomach—
blood started gushing from the man's mouth.
Screaming, he fell down.
But the SS guard kept kicking him—
in his face, his head, his groin, his legs,
until one last brutal kick in the pit of his stomach
and the victim lay twitching
and finally inert in a pool of blood.

Attack Dogs

brutal SS guard dogs
were everywhere—

barking & instilling fear
in new arrivals—

guarding the gates
& the crematoriums—

sinking their fangs
into any unlucky *Häftling*

who lagged behind
in the work detail—

Karl Franz
commandant of Treblinka

set his dog on the Jews
to bite off their genitals—

just for fun
sadistic guards

sent their dogs
to kill a prisoner—

SS dogs were even known
to eat a prisoner—

after liberation
several prisoners

killed & ate
the dogs.

SS Sport

you must crouch
and jump
with heavy stones
in your arms

you must run
hour after hour
while carrying
heavy stones

you must crawl
on your elbows and toes
rolling over ground
covered with glass
and broken bricks

you must
walk on salt
after the soles
of your feet
are gashed

all day you must
stand up lie down
stand up lie down
amidst kicking
hitting yelling—
dying

all "sport" exercises
must be performed
at a brisk pace
including singing
while marching.

In Step
March
Sing

singing songs
in the camps
was part of
the daily
routine—
they sang
while marching
to & from work
sang while
doing exercises
sang during
forced labor
sang during
roll call
sang
for
punishments
sang during
beatings
sang for
executions—
any *Häftling*
who didn't
know the song
was beaten—
anyone who
sang too soft
was beaten—
anyone who
didn't keep time
was beaten—
the whole block
would sing—

small groups
would sing—
they sang for
hour after hour
'til they couldn't
sing another note.

Another SS Sport— Walking a Straight Line

your
life
depends
on
your
walking
straight
in
a
straight
line
while
SS
bullets
whizz
by
on
both
sides
of
the
line.

Excursion Fares

Someone had to pay for the Jews
to ride in the boxcars:
the *Reichsbahn* demanded payment
by the track kilometer.
So the Gestapo, Eichmann's office,
paid for one-way fares, group rate,
guards were charged for the round-trip,
children under ten rode for half-fare,
children under four rode free.

Jumpers

the only hope for a few
to escape

was to jump from the
death trains—

naked, in sub-freezing
winter

they jumped—

suffocating from the heat,
packed like sardines,

their feet burning from the lime
coating the floor

they jumped—

some escaped,
most jumpers were shot

by the Ukrainian
guards.

Fox-Trots and Tangos

In Belzec the orchestra played
between the gas chamber and mass grave.
Day after day flutes and fiddles
and harmonicas taken from the dead
they played.

In Birkenau in mid-1944, an orchestra
of young women in white blouses
and navy skirts played for new arrivals.

In Auschwitz the beat of big drums
and cymbals kept prisoners marching
to and from work. Sunday concerts
for the Commandant, in front of his villa
they played. They played for speeches.
In clean white suits they played
for visitors, played for transports,
played to entertain the SS, played
for hangings.

Fox-trots and tangos. *The Merry Widow.*
The *Barcarolle* from *The Tales of Hoffmann.*
Marches. Popular German songs.
Lilting, cheerful melodies they played.

After Injecting a Woman

After injecting a woman with a shot of phenol
to the heart,

Dr. Mengele hands the sick card
to an attendant:

"*Herzanfall* (heart attack)."

White Powder

In the kitchen
SS women
measure out
white powder
into the
camp soup—
we think it's
some sort
of Bromide*
says Kitty Hart—
you get diarrhea
slow down
become confused—
is this what
stops us
from menstruating?
worried it would
turn us
into *Muselmänner*
we suspect
something—
the soup smelled
revolting—
but we were
desperate
we drank the stuff.

Avo research showed this was poison.

Selekeja

undress

make sure
you have
a card

with
your
number—

walk naked
past the
SS man—

you must
go to the
left

or
to the
right—

left
is the
side

of
the
condemned—

if
your number
is taken

you will be
given

a double
ration

before
deporting

for the
gas.

Nachtwache

the children are calling,
the one, three, five,
and seven-year-old children
are calling tonight from Mengele's
special barracks.

they are calling this word *Nachtwache*,
which they must learn even before
they learn to say *Mama*,
a word they may never
have to learn.

they are calling
for the night watchman to come
before they urinate.
will the children pee
before their calls
are answered?

if the children don't call,
or the night watchman
doesn't come,
and they soil themselves,
then in the morning
they will be taken.

Death by Flogging

eins
zwei
drei
vier
fünf

twenty-five blows
on the
bare buttock
with a whip
or wooden club

sechs
sieben
acht
neun
zehn

twenty-five blows
was the minimum—
the *Häftling* had to
count each blow
aloud

elf
zwölf
dreizehn
vierzehn
fünfzehn

if he failed
to keep count
the flogging started again
from the
beginning

eins
zwei
drei
vier
fünf

The Pillar

Suspended
from *The Pillar*

with his hands
tied behind his back

with his feet unable
to touch the ground

the *Häftling*
is suspended for hours

he loses consciousness
from the pain

suspension tears
his arm tendons

so how could he walk?
if you can't walk

it meant death.

Goebbels Calendar

every Jewish holiday
every Saturday, *Shabbos*,
the infirmary is emptied,
the sick are taken—
the block of *Muselmänner*
are taken to the gas.
in Auschwitz the *Häftlinge*
call this "Goebbels Calendar."

on the Day of Atonement
September 30, 1944,
a group of young boys
are forced by Mengele
to walk under a plank—
those not tall enough
to reach the board over
their heads, are "selected."
a thousand boys
on Yom Kippur—
"Goebbels Calendar."

We Cried All Night

You're not pure Aryan,
you're a Gypsy.
You're mixed blood—*de Mishlinga*,
never to mix with the German *Volk*.
You're a thief, beggar, swindler.
You're lazy, unreliable.
You're disturbed.
You're unbalanced.
You're a parasite.
You're a Gypsy plague.

So they took us to the ghetto,
to Lodz, to Warsaw,
took us to the camps,
to Chełmno, Treblinka, Dachau,
Belzec, Majdanek,
Ravensbrück, Mauthausen,
Buchenwald.
To Auschwitz, to Mengele they took us.
And we cried all night
that night the violins stopped playing,
that night we shared the fate
of the Jews.

Loot

it took
> more than
>> an hour

for a column
> of baby carriages
>> five abreast

to pass by
> Wanda Saynik
>> in Auschwitz.

Fried Noodles Topped with Raisins Cinnamon and Vanilla Cream

For Nina Pächter
and the women of Terezín.

Make a noodle dough from ½ kilogram flour,
2 eggs, 2–3 tablespoons white wine,
2–3 tablespoons thick sour cream...

We dig through the garbage heaps
rotting in the courtyard,
eat our watery pea powder soup,
our gray bread and potato peels.
But here in Terezín
we feed our minds with favorite recipes,
getting each ingredient just right, even arguing,
"cooking with the mouth."

Next, roll out the dough medium thick.
Cut short noodles and fry them in hot fat...

No eggs. No butter, cream, noodles.
But our recipes have them.
And we, the women of Terezín, have them as weapons
against a constant hunger. We write them
on scraps of paper, one of them across a picture
of Hitler.

Remove the noodles and put them into a
soufflé dish. Sprinkle them with sugar,
cinnamon and many raisins...

We fight back with Chocolate Strudel, with
Chicken Galantine garnished with aspic and caviar,
with Goose Neck stuffed with Farina, Goulash with
Noodles, Potato Herring, Nut Braid topped with
sugar icing, Liver Dumplings, Apple Dumplings,
Farina Dumplings, Cherry-Plum Dumplings, and

Mrs. Weil's Viennese Dumplings you can serve plain
or with roasts. Rye Schnapps, Macaroons, Linzer
Torte, Ice Cream à la Melba, Bean Cake, Czech Cake,
Butter Kindelin, and Cheap Real Jewish Bobe.

Now make a delicate vanilla cream, add a little
raw cream and pour over fried noodles.
Bake a little. Bring to table in dish.

Jewish Bullets

Tuvia Borzykowski
recalls a number of Jews
were being deported
along the street
in the Warsaw Ghetto.
suddenly a small group of Jews
led by Mordechai Anielewicz
began to throw grenades
at the German guards and SS.
several of the Germans fell.
others ran away—
the fighters
set up a barricade
in a little house on Niska Street
and held it against
the German reinforcements,
firing until the bullets ran out.
the Germans set the house on fire—
the Jews were destroyed.
but for the first time
Germans stood in fear
of being hit
by a Jewish bullet.

The shots began the largest single act of Jewish resistance during the Holocaust.
                                                                    —Marci Shore

Aflame

Teletype message
Warsaw Ghetto Operation
22 April 1943

Our setting the block on fire achieved the result in the course of the night that those Jews whom we had not been able to find despite all our search operations left their hideouts under the roofs, in the cellars, and elsewhere, and appeared at the outside of the buildings, trying to escape the flames. Masses of them—entire families—were already aflame and jumped from the windows or endeavored to let themselves down by means of sheets tied together or the like. Steps had been taken so that these Jews as well as the remaining ones were liquidated at once. During the whole night there were shots from buildings which were supposed to be evacuated. We had no losses in our cordoning forces. 5,300 Jews were caught for the evacuation and removed.

The SS & Police Führer in the district of Warsaw. Signed: Stroop

The Last Jew

"The Warsaw ghetto is no more."
—German commander, General Stroop

Back through the sewers I slog,
back to the ghetto,

walk for hours in the ruins,
go from bunker to bunker,

yell the password: *Jan*,
says Simba Rotten.

Smoke. Smell of charred flesh.

From the rubble
a woman calling, calling.

I search, can't find her.

Except for her voice
I'm alone. Not another soul.

I say to myself
I'm the last Jew.

Shattering the Silence:
1943 Gallup Poll
Asks Americans

it is said that
two million Jews*

have been killed
in Europe

since the war
began.

is this true
or just a rumor?

47% true

29% rumor

24% no opinion

---

*Allied leadership publicly confirmed that two million Jews had been murdered.

What About the Jews, FDR?

The State Department
& Downing Street

avert their eyes
from the slaughter

you, Mr. President,
must take the lead

the time is now.

From an editorial by Max Lerner in the New York PM.

Dying Notes

Janowska—
the notes
of the
camp orchestra
dying
along with
all the players
shot
while standing
in a circle
playing
their final
concert.

Letter to God
from a Child in Izieu

God? How good You are, how kind,
and if one had to count the number of goodnesses
and kindnesses You have done,
one would never finish.

God? It is You who command.
You who reward the good and punish the evil.
God? It is thanks to You
that I had a beautiful life before.

God? I ask You one thing only:
make my parents come back,
my poor parents. Protect them
(even more than you protect me)

so that I can see them again
as soon as possible.
Make them come back again.
Ah! I had such a good mother

and such a good father!
I have such faith in You
and I thank You
in advance.

Eleven-year-old Liliane Gerenstein wrote this letter to God just days before she, her brother, and all 44 Jewish children sheltered in the orphanage known as La Maison d'Izieu were sent to their deaths at Auschwitz along with their supervisors. Only one supervisor out of seven survived.

Got Mit Uns

God
is with us

says
the belt buckle

on the
SS uniform.

Muselmänner

nose running into mouth
diarrhea running into rags
rags running with lice
eyes blank, bulging
head dropped, wagging
arms skeletal
feet swollen
aimless shuffle
walking death.

To Wash

if you don't bother
to wash your face
with a fistful of snow

or take a few swallows
of the morning coffee
using the rest to wash—

if you feel washing's
a waste of time
and stop—

you could be
taking the first step
to the grave—

to wash is an
expression
of life.

Organize

Organize was the most important word
in the Auschwitz language.
—Auschwitz survivor

you didn't live long
      in Auschwitz

if you didn't exchange
      or *organize*—

food, clothing,
      your shoes *organized*

your spoon & bowl
      organized

one couldn't survive
      without them—

an additional sip
      of coffee

a better sleeping place on
      the three-tiered planks

medicine, drugs,
      your job

even sabotage
      could be *organized*

everything *organized*
      was paid for with bread

in the *lager*
      bread was money.

The Bread Law

From the evening ration we laid by
bits of bread for the next day.
It was a life-preserver, says Leon Szalet.

People grew pale and collapsed
when they realized their piece was stolen.
A wrong done to all of us,
says Jorge Semprun.
Suspicion, distrust, hate settled in.

So what happened when a bread thief
was caught? We killed him.
What's the use of beating up a bastard
like that? That was the law
in Block 18, says Rudolph Vrba.
If you weren't strong enough to carry out
the sentence, others take care of him.

Piled High

every
morning
after
Appell
they
piled
the
night's
dead
in
front
of
each
Block—
naked
emaciated
skeletons
piled
high
waiting
for
the
Leichenkommando—
waiting
for
the
cremo.

Handing the Dead
to Each Other

they called them
the *Leichenkommando*—
the corpse squad.

In the women's barracks
in Auschwitz their job
was to load the dead
into trucks.

one woman *Häftling*
stood near a pile of corpses,
a second stood near the truck,
the third on a small stool,
and the fourth
on the truck's platform.

"they handed the dead
to each other any old way,"
said Sara Nomberg-Przytyk.

"they just grabbed a corpse
by the leg or arm or hair
and swung it onto the platform.

every few minutes
one could hear the thump
of falling flesh."

Pregnant Women

beaten
with clubs
whips
torn by dogs
dragged around
by the hair
kicked in the stomach—
when they collapse
says Gisella Pearl
they're thrown
into the crematory
alive.

6,000 Lethal Volts—
The Power to Liberate

in the morning in Birkenau
a special detail
with hooked sticks
detach the deformed bodies
that had run on the wire—
we were sorry for them
said Olga Lengyel
yet we envied them—
they had the courage
to relieve themselves
of their misery
the courage to reject life
which no longer
merited the name.

Surprise Soup

in the *lager* the guards and cooks
take the best share of food.

what we get, says Olga Lengyel,
is bread made partly of sawdust

and a soup made of thistles or worse.
we call it *surprise soup*—

it comes with unexpected
surprising ingredients:

buttons, keys, tufts of hair,
dead mice—

once we were treated
to a small metal sewing kit

complete with needles
and thread.

The Others

you must stick together.
you must not be
separated from your group.

the others will carry you
and prop you up with their bodies
when you can't stand for *appell.*

when you're cold the others
will shield you with their bodies
from the blowing wind.

dying from thirst?
the others in your work group
will stand watch for you
as you lap up a lifesaving
drink of water from the stream.

the others will help you
organize a spoon or a pair of shoes
bring you some bread
a little honey
a carrot.

the others will tell you
you've got to wash
somehow.

getting weaker?
the others will steer you
to a *Kommando* where the guards
aren't strict and the work
not too heavy.

isolated or alone
you'll never make it—
you'll never survive without
the others.

We All Know What Mengele Does with Women Who Have Babies in Camp,

so births take place in secrecy
in the block where we live,
says Sara Nomberg-Przytyk.
After birth, we kill the baby
by injection, then tell the mother
her baby's born dead.
After dark, we throw the baby
on a pile of corpses.
That way, we save the mother.

Vanilla Ice-Cream

From the diary of
SS Dr. Johann Kremer

5 September 1942:
this noon was present in a special action
in the women's camp
(the selection and gassing of
800 emaciated women).

men compete to take part in such actions
as they get additional rations—
one fifth litre vodka,
five cigarettes,
one hundred grams of sausage
and bread.

6 September 1942:
today an excellent Sunday dinner:
tomato soup, one half of chicken with potatoes
and red cabbage (20 grams of fat),
dessert and magnificent
vanilla ice-cream.

Thirst

lips parched
splitting
gums swollen
tongue swollen
no saliva
mouth
ulcers
bleeding
can't eat
can't speak
can't close
your mouth
can't hear
can't see
eyes burning
are you going
blind from
thirst?

Morgen Früh

Do you know how one says never
in camp slang? Morgen früh:
tomorrow morning.

     —Primo Levi

Will you wake on a plank of wood
with six others,
wash your face in your morning coffee,
and go to work in the mud?
Tomorrow morning.

Will you go to the latrine when
they tell you,
or be shot at roll call
because you did it in your pants?
Tomorrow morning.

Tomorrow morning
the boils and pus and lice
will be gone,
the blue tattoo will fade from your wrist,
the green dye will fade from your eyes,
the sweet singed smell
will fade from your nostrils.

Tomorrow morning
they'll give you back your ovaries,
give you back your children,
give you back your old wool coat
with the yellow star,
and you'll give them back
the paper cement bag
stuffed under your dress.

Tomorrow morning
you'll run a comb
through your long black hair,
tie it with a bright red ribbon,

197

and someone will smile and say:
Good morning, Lena.

Tomorrow morning
there'll be no more ashes
to fill the swamp
to dump in the river
to fertilize the fields. No more ashes
to spread on the paths like gravel
under the boots of the SS.

Tomorrow morning.
Tomorrow morning.
Morgen früh.

The Waiting Room
for the Crematoria
Is Emptied

ambulances and trucks
are stopping in front of the *KaBe*.

all the sick are being taken
to the gas.

the SS are beating and kicking
the patients.

blood, nothing but blood
everywhere, says Olga Lengyel.

blood on the floor, the walls,
the SS uniforms, their boots.

as we gather the scattered blankets
and basins and instruments

we knew it was our turn
next.

Meanwhile, Back in America,
It's Spike Jones and His City Slickers Band

When der Führer says we is de master race
        We *heil* right in der Führer's face

Not to love der Führer is a great disgrace
        So we *heil heil* right in der Führer's face...

This is a version of Oliver Wallace's theme song released January, 1943. The song parodied the Nazi anthem "Horst Weesel Lied."

Black Sun

tall chimney
       roaring

belching red
       & black

sun black

a black shroud
       hanging

over our
       graves

somewhere
       in the sky.

Mengele's Music

whistling Mozart, the *Blue Danube Waltz,*
a favorite Puccini aria,

Mengele conducts his *selektion*
before the baths—

his baton beating
beating

left right
life death.

To Scream

in Auschwitz
a girl starts screaming
in her sleep—
suddenly
our entire barrack
joins her
says Sarah Berkowitz.
we're screaming
this endless scream
in horror
without knowing
why?
are we screaming
to the outside world
for help?
we unlearned
to laugh
we can't cry anymore—
if nothing else is left
one must scream

aghaaaaaaaaaaaaaaaaaah

Another *Muselmann*

Their life was short
but their number was endless.

—Primo Levi

you keep talking keep on telling him it's not too late
even though his eyes are blank you keep on talking
but he doesn't hear you he shuffles off dragging his feet

you keep talking but that bleary look is still in his eyes
you give him a piece of bread but even food does not
interest him he has given up *you must keep going* you shout

you keep talking but he doesn't have the strength
to dodge the dogs to dodge the blows he doesn't have
the strength to throw himself on the electric fence

you keep talking but his head is loose wagging
you see he looks like a living skeleton you see he is
doomed you keep talking but you see he is a *Muselmann*.

The Last Batch

Barrack 25. The death block.
It stood apart from the rest of Birkenau.
Barred windows. A single gate
guarded day and night. A brick wall
surrounding the courtyard, surrounding
sobs and groans of women waiting for the gas,
naked women who hadn't been fed for days.
Seweyna Szmaglewska recalls figures
like mannequins hobbling onto the trucks,
pressing into each other. She recalls
the last batch, who couldn't stand,
being thrown one on top of another.
Remembers the trucks speeding by,
bodies rocking with every jolt,
thin legs and arms rising and falling
in unison, waving, waving.

The Burning Pits

too many Hungarian Jews
for the ovens

so behind crematorium V
they dug pits

piled one on top
of the other

set fire to the bodies
both dead and alive

poured the rendered fat
over them

so everyone could
burn better.

Almost one half of all the Jews that were killed in Auschwitz were Hungarian Jews
who were gassed within a period of 10 weeks in 1944. The burning pits were ablaze
day and night. 46,000 people were being annihilated every day.

Proposal for Collecting Jewish Skulls

after the Jew is put to death
without injuring his skull
the physician severs the head
then sends it to the lab in a tin box
as soon as it's received
record on a photographic plate the results
to define racial features
based on the shape of the skull
the shape and size
of the brain
etc.

The Natzweiler concentration camp set up this program.

Profit Per Prisoner

Based on a life expectancy of nine months,
the SS estimated the profit from the average
concentration camp prisoner: $645.00
(after deducting upkeep).

Adding in money, valuables, clothing,
personal belongings, plus teeth of precious
metals, they came up with another $91.00
(after deducting costs for burning the body).

According to Nazi calculations, the total
profit from one prisoner (not including the
value of bones and ashes used as fill and
fertilizer) came to 1,631 *Reichsmarks*,
$745.00.

Restaurant
Ticket Office
Telegraph & Telephone

on the building where
the victims clothing is stored,

fake station signs greet the Jews
at Treblinka:

schedules announce trains:
Grodno, Suwalki, Vienna, Berlin:

huge signposts say
To Bialystok and Baranowicze:

an enormous arrow says
Change for Eastbound Trains:

the clock's hands frozen
at midnight.

In Treblinka
on "The Road to Heaven"

When they need
to slow down traffic,
a Ukrainian opens a booth,
collects "one zloty to
pay for the bath."

When traffic needs
speeding up
they tell the Jews:
"hurry up, before
the water gets cold."

Arbeit Macht Frei*

work never freed
anyone

who passed under
this gate

into Auschwitz.

---

*Work Makes You Free.

The Death Haircut

in the undressing room in Treblinka
women had their hair cut—

"we just cut their hair with scissors
and a comb, without any clippers,"

said Abraham Bomba.

"we made them believe
they were getting a nice haircut,

just like a man's,

so they should not know
they're going to be gassed—

it took about two minutes,
not even two minutes, because

the next group was waiting
to come in."

Treblinka Greetings

looking up,
one couldn't miss
the Star of David

underneath the gable
on the front wall
of the gas chamber.

on entering,
a dark synagogue curtain
offers greetings
in Hebrew:

This is the gate
through which
the righteous pass.

The Pink Triangle

you're vermin.
you're socially aberrant.
you're a cancerous ulcerous tumor.
you're an antisocial parasite, a race defiler,
an enemy of the state.

you're a 175er: a homosexual degenerate.
you debilitate the Aryan *Volk.*
you threaten disciplined masculinity.
you're an infection turning into an epidemic.
you're a filthy queer, a shitty queer arse-hole.

you're a pervert, the scum of humanity,
a butt-fucker.
you're guilty of the "syphilization
of the German people."
you will be exterminated root and branch
like the Jews.

so they took us to the camps:
to Dachau, Flossenbürg, Neuengamme.
took us to Buchenwald,
Sachsenhausen, Mauthausen,
Natzweiler-Stutthof.
took us to Oranienburg,
to Dora-Mittelbau,
to Melk, to Ebensee.

the pink triangle
marked us for medical experiments,
marked us for work in the clay pits,
the "death pits."

marked us as targets "shot trying to escape."
marked us for a *kapo*'s lover, a "dolly boy."
if we lived long enough,
we had a choice:
we could be castrated,
or sent to the Eastern front.

---

*Homosexuals released at the end of the war were not liberated, their persecution
continued under the allies and the German authorities.*

In the Mines

in the mines
they worked to death
starved to death—
a meal consisted of
a bowl of hot water
and a handful
of urine.

Jewish Slaves

in Budapest
Jews caught in the street
in an *Aktia*
were placed in a labor battalion.

badly fed and poorly clothed
they dug anti-tank ditches
laid railroad track
built roads
buried their dead Jews.

they got beatings
they got less and less food
they got sleepless nights
they starved to death
froze to death.

forced to slide down a mountain
on their stomachs—
pushed to their deaths
off cliffs—

used as living mine detectors
Jews were ordered
to march into the minefield
to clear the area
for the regular troops.

One Pair of Men's Trousers, Used, 3 *Reichsmarks*

First they took the shops, businesses,
factories. Then they took the jewelry, radios,
furs. Dogs and cats they took.

Then belongings in the death camps piled up.
In Auschwitz, it took several dozen barracks
to hold them. (They called it *Canada*.)

What to do with it? SS Lieutenant-General
August Frank had the answer. In a note to the
head of the Lublin region and to Auschwitz

on September 26, 1942, he said: foreign
currency, jewels, pearls, gold teeth were to
be delivered to the *Reichsbank*.

Watches, clocks, pens, electric razors, hand
razors, pocket knives, scissors, flashlights,
wallets and purses were to be cleaned,

evaluated, then delivered to front line troops.
Then, offered for sale. No officer or soldier
could buy more than one watch. Proceeds go

to the *Reich*. Gold watches to the SS.
Underwear and footwear were sorted, valued,
given to Ethnic Germans. Pure silk underwear

was sent to the *Reich Ministry of Economics*.
Quilts, blankets, thermoses, earflaps, combs,
knives, forks, spoons, sheets, pillows, towels,

tablecloths were for Ethnic Germans. Eyeglasses
for the Medical Office of the army. Gold frames
and valuable furs for the SS. Prices must be

established. For instance, "one pair of used men's trousers, 3 *Reichsmarks*, one woolen blanket, 6 *Reichsmarks*," etc. It must be

strictly observed that the Jewish star is removed from all garments. All items should be searched for hidden valuables sewn in.

The Purple Triangle

We are Jehovah's Witnesses—
the Germans call us *Bibelforscher*—Bible students.
We are the resisters. We will not Heil Hitler.
Our children in school will not Heil Hitler.
We will not join the Nazi party
or fly the German flag—the swastika.
We will not serve in military training
or the *Wehrmacht.*
We will not work for anything
that contributes to the war effort.
We refuse to renounce our religious faith
and refuse to support Hitler's regime.
We hold steadfast to our religious convictions
based on the Bible.
So our children they took from us
and sent us to the camps—
to Bergen-Belsen, Buchenwald, Sachsenhausen,
Ravensbrück, Mauthausen,
To Auschwitz they took us
and marked us with a purple triangle.
And we treated our imprisonment
as the fulfillment of the will of God.

It is estimated that 2,500 to 5,000 Witnesses died in the camps—about 200 more were executed for refusing military service.

Among the Dresses and Underwear,

mothers hide their babies
at the last minute
with the hope that once inside
they'll remain together.
but all luggage is taken.
by the time the bags
are opened for sorting in Canada*
the children are dead.

Huts in which packages and suitcases were unpacked and sorted for dispatch to Germany.

Toothpaste

In Canada, while sorting
the loot of Auschwitz victims,

Rudolph Vrba recalls seeing
"girls straddling a bench,

squeezing tubes of toothpaste
onto the bench. It seemed

to verge on lunacy,
for I had yet to learn that

one tube in ten thousand
maybe had a diamond in it—

a nest egg some family hoped
might buy their freedom."

From the Interrogation of Adolf Eichmann

a sealed van drew up
naked Jews had to get inside—

I followed the van
it drove up to a long trench—

doors opened
bodies were thrown out—

they seemed alive
their limbs were so supple—

a civilian pulled out teeth with some pliers—
then I got the hell out of there

I was too upset
I'd had more than I could take.

In a Train
Arriving in Treblinka
from Kielce,

at least half were dead—
they had slashed their wrists
or just died—
the ones they unloaded were half dead
half mad—
they piled them—thousands—
one on top of another
on the ramp, stacked
like wood.

Figuren

Figuren: figures, puppets, marionettes

The Germans ordered all bodies
in mass graves dug up and burned.
They started with the oldest graves in Vilna,
the first ghetto. They open the graves
without tools. As they dig down,
the flatter the bodies.

Szloma Gol found his brother
at the Polnar pits outside Vilna.
"He'd been dead already two years
when I dug him up."

Isaac Dognim recognized
his wife, three sisters, three nieces.
He knew it was his wife
because she wore the wedding medallion
he'd given her.

Another *Special Commando 1005* at Ponar
built log pyres, dug up corpses,
threw them on pyres, and scattered the ashes.
Each pyre held 3,500 bodies. They burnt
for ten days. Bones were ground to powder,
taken away in sacks.

In Vilna, anyone who said "corpse"
was beaten. They had to call bodies
Figuren.

Death by Beheading

In Sobibor, a captain from Holland, a Jew,
began plotting an uprising.
The Germans found out and began questioning him
to find out the ringleaders. This man withstood tortures
and endless blows and he never said a word.
Told if he didn't speak, the Dutch blocks
would be beheaded in front of his eyes.
He said "you'll never get a word out of me."
The Germans kept their word—
about seventy Dutch people were beheaded.
Yes, they cut off their heads.

Dov Freiberg, Sobibor Survivor

Last Words of a Young Girl
from *Sonderkommando* Salem Lewenthal's Ms.
Found Buried in a Jar in Birkenau
Near Crematorium III

I am still so young,
I have not
experienced anything
in my life.
why should death
of this kind
fall to my lot?
why?
one should
like so much
to live
a little longer.

Producing Dead Women

When we left work, we would take the dead
woman's bodies on our shoulders and carry them
to the crematoria. The SS men beat us

demanding that we carry them well.
But we were so weak we couldn't work on our feet
from such a day's work on a half liter of soup.

The guard delivered lectures to us:
"You dirty Jews, you who deprived us of bread
for years, you have become rich,

you have everything, gorging yourselves
with food and drink. And now we have
brought you here to punish you.

The crematoria are too good for you.
We shall make you croak little by little.
You will plead for death, but death

will not come so soon. Death would be
too good a thing for you."
We were beaten until twelve o'clock.

The SS man who could prove
that he had produced dead women
was considered a good worker.

He mastered his trade well.

Edith S., Testimony, 1946.

Murder by Suicide—
Buchenwald Quarry

A prisoner was told to lie down
and pull down his trousers.
He's given 25 blows so he can't get up—
then he's hit in the face
so he's entirely covered with blood.

If he's not dead
he has to carry a large stone
from the quarry. If he can't walk
he's hit on the head and hands
where he holds the stone.
If the stone falls from his hands
he's again beaten.

All day we had to run up and down
with stones. When we got up
there with large stones and put them down,
we had to run down into the quarry
on the double. The German *kapos*
and SS men beat us day in, day out.

We had no hope of holding out
and sought death.
The sentries would shoot everybody
who came near them
or who wanted to run through,
or were forced by the *kapos* to seek death
because it was too hard—

many of us were murdered,
murdered by suicide.

Bernard W., Testimony, 1946.

Death March

We eat everything
that's green or alive.
We eat grass.
We eat leaves.
We peel bark off trees.
We swallow live little frogs.
Nettles we eat.

Some boiled potatoes
a lady tosses—
put one in your mouth
and you'll taste a bullet.

We suck the earth,
lick dew off rocks,
scoop a little snow for a drink.

We march for hours,
march for weeks,
in a zigzag pattern we march.
In rain, snow,
half barefoot in frost we march.

We stumble.
We lag behind.
We seek the ditch.
We fall.
We get up.
We can't get up.
We keep going.

Every few minutes a shot.

Approximately a hundred thousand Jews died on the death marches in 1944–45, when the Germans, knowing they would be defeated, evacuated the concentration camps.

The Gardelegen Massacre

April 18, 1945—
      time is running out for the Nazis—
the Red Army & the American Army
      are closing in—

needing a quick way to kill over
      a thousand prisoners
the Nazis find it
      in a large brick barn—

young boys in SS uniforms
      Luftwaffe soldiers under the direction
of a *Wehrmacht* soldier
      round up over a thousand prisoners

herd them into the barn
      douse it with gasoline & set it on fire—
those that try to escape the inferno
      are machine gunned to death—

the Germans attempt
      to destroy the evidence
burying the bodies in mass graves
      in front of the barn—

the following day American soldiers
      discover the atrocity—
over a thousand charred
      burnt bodies.

The prisoners were evacuated from the Dora-Mittelbau camp and some of its sub-camps. The massacre took place near the medieval German town of Gardelegen.

Part Five: Liberation

For Most of It I Have No Words

From Edward R. Murrow's radio broadcast
after visiting Buchenwald: April 15, 1945

There surged around me an evil smelly stink, men and boys
reached out to touch me. They were in rags and remnants of
uniforms. Death already had marked many of them...I asked
to see one of the barracks...men crowded around...many of them
could not get out of bed. I was told this building once stabled
80 horses. There were 1200 men in it, five to a bunk. The stink
was beyond description...as we walked out a man fell dead.
They showed me the children. Some were only six years old.
I could see their ribs through their thin shirts. One rolled up
his sleeves, showed me his number. It was tattooed on his arm.
B-6030, it was. The others showed me their numbers. They will
carry them with them till they die. We went to the hospital.
The doctor told me that 200 had died the day before. I asked the
cause of death. He shrugged and said: "Tuberculosis, starvation,
fatigue, and there are many who have no desire to live."
He pulled back the blanket from a man's feet to show me how
swollen they were. The man was dead. We proceeded to what had
been a stable or garage. We entered. There were two rows
of bodies stacked like cordwood. They were thin and very white.
Some of the bodies were terribly bruised, though there seemed
to be little flesh to bruise. Some had been shot through the head,
but they bled but little. I arrived at the conclusion that all
that was mortal of more than 500 men and boys lay there in two
neat piles...the clothing was piled in a heap against the wall.
It appeared that most of the men and boys had died of starvation,
they had not been executed. But the manner of death seemed
unimportant. Murder had been done at Buchenwald. God alone
knows how many men and boys have died there...I was told that
there were more than 20,000 in the camp. There had been
as many as 60,000. Where are they now? I pray you to believe
what I have said about Buchenwald. I reported what I saw
and heard, but only part of it. For most of it, I have no words.
If I have offended you by this rather mild account of Buchenwald,
I'm not in the least sorry.

From a Letter by Delbert Cooper, a Soldier
with the U.S. 71st Infantry Division

While we stood outside the truck,
any number of them came up
and touched us, as if they couldn't
believe we were actually there.
Some of them would try to kiss us even.
They must have been bad off.
Some of them would grab you around the neck
and cry on your shoulder.
Others would just look and cry.
Some of them would throw their arms
up in the air and pray,
the ones who were too weak to stand.
I recall one woman who could only cry
and point at her mouth.
One fellow felt that he should give me
something. So, as he had nothing,
he gave me his little yellow star
that designates a Jew.
I'll send it to you another letter.

Gunskirchen

a strong
nauseating
smell

greeted
the
G.I.'s

liberating
the Gunskirchen
camp—

dead
decaying
bodies

lying
everywhere—

lying in
their own
feces

& urine
& pulpy
mud.

Just three miles from Gunskirchen American troops found a food warehouse stocked with dried noodles, potatoes, soups, meats & other foods.

A Dozen Bodies
in a Dirty Boxcar,

at liberation at Dachau.
men and women.

they had gone so long
without food, says Bill Barrett,

their wrists were broomsticks
with claws.

Chocolate Bar Death

in the camps
on the day
of liberation
emaciated
starved survivors
were so hungry
they ate the cigarettes
handed out
they ate army rations
dried milk powder
oatmeal sugar
salt tinned meat
rich fatty food
chocolate bars
they ate
too fast they ate
dying in
agony.

The Real Criminal—
Last Words from
the Führer Bunker

...that race, Jewry,
is the real criminal
of this murder's struggle...
above all I charge
the leaders of the nation
and those under them
to the scrupulous observance
of the laws of our race
and to merciless opposition
to the universal
prisoner of all peoples,
International Jewry.

From Hitler's last will and testament signed in the Führer Bunker April 29, 1945 a day before his suicide—his will expressed many of the same sentiments he had stated in 1923–24 in Mein Kampf, *"my struggle."*

Filming Dachau with an Eye
to Establish Evidence
That the Showers
Were Not Showers At All

Caption Sheet:

Note airtight door.

Note absence of means
       of opening door from within.

Note absence of rust or oxidation.

Note the bodies that lay sprawled
       awaiting incineration.

Note the ovens were obviously
       in process of being used

at the moment of interruption…
       unswept of bodies and ashes.

Get shot of interior of oven.

———————————————

Lt. Colonel George Stevens, of the U.S. Army Signal Corps, entered Dachau with his film crew the day after liberation, April 30, 1945. The films were used as evidence at the Nuremberg Trials.

For All of Those Who Say
the Holocaust Never Happened

The things I saw beggar description…
the starvation, cruelty and bestiality
were so overpowering
as to leave me a bit sick.
In one room they were piled up
twenty or thirty naked men
killed by starvation.
George Patton would not even enter.
He said he would get sick if he did so.
I made the visit deliberately,
in order to be in a position to give
first-hand evidence of these things,
if in the future there develops
a tendency to charge these allegations
merely to "propaganda."

General Dwight D. Eisenhower in a letter on June 12, 1945 to General Marshall after visiting the Ohrdruf camp near Weimar, Germany—the first Nazi concentration camp liberated by U.S. troops.

Doorsteps

John Fuchs went back to Tszyn.
All the buildings
where the Jews lived were gone.
All the Jews were gone.
The Jewish cemetery where generations
were buried was gone.
The gravestones used for doorsteps.

They Didn't Even Use Bullets

Made it back to Zasów
where I was born,
says Joe Klein,
back to the place
they came to kill me:
standing where my bones
were meant to lie,
remembering:
for the small children
they didn't even
use bullets,
just took by the legs
the babies,
hit their heads
against the trees and
threw them in.

Why Did You Jews Have to Come Back from the Dead While Most of the Others Disappeared?

Back to Lublin,
back from the dead,

Maria Ezner walks into the house
where she once lived.

Looted. Empty.
No bed. No table. No chairs.

Nothing.

Nail holes by the door
where the *mezuzah* hung.

So, you're still alive.
Clear out or else…

Where Did They Come From, the Jews?
The Devil, I Never Knew So Many of Them
Were Left Alive?

The war is over.
But not the war against the Jews.
Jews continue to be murdered
by Poles.
A Jew returning to Choroszeza
is taken from a train
and beaten to death.

Jewish survivors returning
to Działoszyce,
determined to rebuild their lives,
are murdered.
Jews are killed by Poles
in Parczew, Turek,
Piotrków, Bolesławiec,
Kosów Lacki.

Jews are killed on a train from Lodz.
Taken out of their cars and shot
in Nowy Targ.
Killed in Krakow, in Sosnowiec.
Killed in their hospital beds
in Lublin.

Jewish orphans are attacked
in a hospital in Radom.
42 Jews who returned to Kielce are shot,
stoned to death, killed with axes,
murdered in their homes,
dragged into the streets and killed
by the mob.

After a year in which
no German soldier was on their soil,
some 350 Jews are killed
in Poland by Poles.

Still
Behind
Barbed Wire

DPs—
Displaced Persons—
they survived the camps
only to find themselves
still in the camps
behind barbed wire.
they had no passports,
no birth certificates,
nowhere to go.
most didn't want to
go back to their countries,
especially Poland,
where their families
had been slaughtered.
maybe they could find
some country or relative
that would be willing
to take them in?

We Do Not
Exterminate Them

The Harrison Report
August 1945

As things stand now,
we appear to be treating the Jews
as the Nazis treated them,
except that we do not exterminate them.
They are in concentration camps
in large numbers under our military guard
instead of SS troops. One is led to wonder
whether the German people seeing this,
are not supposing that we are following
or at least condoning Nazi policy.

---

*President Harry Truman anxious to appease concerns sent Earl G. Harrison to
investigate the DP camps. All the DP camps were finally closed in 1957.*

Part Six: Afterwards

Evidence

*Affidavit presented at the
International Military Tribunal
at Nuremberg.*

I declare herewith under oath
that in the years 1941 to 1943

during my tenure in office as a commandant
of Auschwitz Concentration Camp

2 million Jews were put to death by gassing
and ½ million by other means.

*Signed,
Rudolf Hoess
May 14, 1946*

Strands

I am the hair shorn and shaved from the skulls
before you pound them to dust to mix with
the ashes flushed into the pond near Birkenau.
I am the hair from under the arms, the hair

from between the legs. I am the hair cut with
the crooked black cross of swastika.
I am the hair without the pins, without the
ribbons, without the lice. I am the hair combed

and packed in the white cloth sack, awaiting
delivery to Alex Zin Fizfabric AG in Roth,
near Nuremberg. I am the hair packed and priced
at one-half *Reichsmark* or $1.09 a kilogram.

I am the hair for socks, the hair for thread,
the hair for ignition for bombs, the hair
for rope for ships, the hair for stuffing
mattresses. I am the hair from Selma and Ida

and Olga and Frida and Berthe.
The hair from Liliane and Simone and Renée
and Hannah. I am the hair from Z-63598.
Look for me behind the glass.

A Stone for Janusz Korczak

Treblinka:
a graveyard without graves,
but with stones:
big stones, small stones, round stones,
jagged pointed stones:
hundreds of stone markers
marking the Polish-Jewish communities
destroyed here:
stones with names like Radom, Lublin,
Bialystok, Kielce, Piotrków, Staszów,
Jedwabne, Warszawa:
but no Vietnam-like memorial
remembers the names
of the 800,000 Jews murdered here,
except for one:
the only stone in Treblinka
named for a person:
Janusz Korczak.

✡

you strived to keep children
from being beaten and starved,
you believed children are people
now, today,
and have a right
to be treated with tenderness,
with respect.
you vowed to uphold the child
to defend his rights,
and when you heard
two blasts of the whistle
and that dreaded call
Alle Juden raus! Alle Juden raus!
you refused to abandon your
orphaned children,
but led them, heads up,
hand-in-hand with the little ones
marching with your flag,
your banner of bright chestnut blossoms
and green meadows
flying with its blue star of David
garnering the salutes of the Jewish police
as you pass through the ghetto
singing your hiking songs
marching in fours
the stormtroopers lashing you
laughing at you—
as you cross over the bridge to the large ghetto
some Poles below shouting, shouting
Goodbye, good riddance Jews!
as you continue marching
with dignity
to the *Umschlagplatz,*
to the cattle cars
to Treblinka.

✡

I'm lighting candles:
a candle for Giena and Romica and Szymonek:
a candle for Eva, Halinka,
and Jakub:
a candle for Mietek and Abus and Zygmus
and Leon and Sami:
a candle for Hanka and Aronek and Hella
and big Hanna and little Hanna:
a candle for Stefa:
and I'm lighting a candle
for the children
you tried to teach the world to love:
for all of them here in Treblinka,
and for you, Old Doctor,
one last candle I'm lighting
as I place a stone
on your stone:

    JANUSZ KORCZAK
    (HENRYK GOLDSZMIT
    AND THE CHILDREN)

Born Henryk Goldszmit in Warsaw in 1878, Janusz Korczak lived as both a Pole and a Jew. He was a physician, educator and a writer who wrote under the pseudonym Janusz Korczak. Seeking to offer deprived children a better way of life, he spent his life trying to create an ideal haven for poor children. He took a vow to uphold the child and defend his rights. Ironically, he believed no cause, no war, was worth depriving children of their natural right to happiness.

130234

for all of those
who lost their names
for a number:
for all of those
who lost their lives
for the star:
for all of those
I leave my number
that is my name
scratched below
my other scratch
of yellow star.
look: on the wall
in the brick
in my barrack
Block 9
Auschwitz:

130234

Camp records show that number 130234 was given to prisoner Jan Wiater, a Jew brought to Auschwitz from Krakow. On July 17, 1943, a package sent to him was returned to the sender.

Anne Frank, *Jood*

you were fifteen that day
they took your clothes,
your hair, your self,

thinking they could
erase your identity
without erasing your words,

your words of hope that
this hatred of the Jews
will be a passing thing.

but it never happened, Anne,
this old hatred turned into
a crooked cross of swastika,

turned into a yellow star
marking you *Jood*
marking you for Auschwitz,

for Bergen-Belsen,
but leaving no marker
for your grave.

On Looking at 2,500 Pictures of French Children Deported in the Cattle Cars from Drancy to Auschwitz

Baby Marceline Kogan, a cowlick in her hair, offers us a
Bonne Année, a good year, as she smiles at us from the Kogan's New
Year's card for 1941: Marceline is deported with her mother, Felicie,
on convoy 45, November 11, 1942.

Liliane Lip sits on a cushion in her birthday suit: Liliane
is 2 when she is separated from her parents and deported alone on
convoy 29, September 7, 1942.

Doris Lewy, ears sticking out, frowning, can't sit still for
the camera: Doris is deported when she is 15 months old, with her
3-month-old baby sister, Nicole, and her father, grandfather, grand-
mother, and her great grandmother, on convoy 72, April 27, 1944.

Sarah Kornfeld sits in the park with her three children,
Hélène, 7, Anna, 6, and Simone, 3: all but Simone wear the yellow
star, all are separated forcibly from their mother and deported on
convoy 25, August 28, 1942.

Jean-Pierre Guckenheimer laughs as he lathers his
father's face with shaving cream: he is deported with his parents
Ernst and Herta, and his grandfather, Markus, on convoy 62,
November 20, 1943.

Bertrand Herz, 14, poses with his sister Francoise, both
are deported on July 30, 1944 from Toulouse to Buchenwald, both
survive, their parents Will and Louise do not.

Aron Muhlstein is immaculate in his foulard tie and
knicker suit, his beret cocked to one side: he wears a *tallith* and
holds his prayer book firmly in both hands: Aron is deported on
convoy 61, October 28, 1943.

George-André Kohn, handsome, in his neat tie and shirt, looks older than his 12 years when he's deported on the last convoy, 79, on August 17, 1944: George-André is taken to the Neuengamme camp, injected with the tuberculin bacillus, and hanged the day before the camp's liberation, in the basement of a Hamburg school.

It Was Their Blood

when
you were shooting
Jewish men,
women and children
did you
have any feelings
for the people?

nein:
my hatred towards Jews
is too great.

✡

and you,
did you have any feelings
about killing
children?

children, yes—
but it was their blood
they were
Jews
they could grow up.

_____

From interviews with former German soldiers from the 1st Infantry Brigade.

In Your *Lager* Dream,

the black sun
turns orange and warm
the stench of the cremo is gone.
the blue tattoo
fades from your wrist.
the green dye
fades from your eyes.
your long black hair is back,
you brush and comb it,
tie it with your favorite ribbon.
the SS man gives you back
your wool coat with the yellow star.
you give him back the paper bag
stuffed under your dress.
he doesn't take your number.
in your dream you're alone.
Appell is gone.
the *Kapo* is gone.
your *Kommando* is gone,
where are the *Häftlinge?*
you scream. and scream.
the loudspeaker blares
Du Jude, kaputt!
the chimney belches red and black.
the guards sing *Deutschland über Alles.*
they sing the *Horst Wessel* song.
in your dream the snow is red.
Arbeit Macht Frei over the gate is red.
your red soup bowl floats. empty.
like iron words.

Bullet Holes

Krulic Wiler went back to Piotrków
where he'd lived. On the door posts
he saw nail holes from *mezuzahs.*
In the synagogue-turned library,
he saw a wall hidden by a curtain,
saw the Ten Commandments painted
on the wall, saw the bullet holes
where the Germans lined up the people:
All I could picture was my mother
and sister standing there.

No Words

We became aware that our language
lacks words to express this offence,
this demolition of man.

　　　　　　—Primo Levi

if every word was once a poem
what is the word, the metaphor, the meaning
for the gas? for the ovens?
for Auschwitz?
if every word was once a poem
what word can explain
the taking of the children?
children with the star
children too young for the star
but not too young
for the bullet
the fire.

Ashes

Sobibor Majdanek Chełmno Belzec Treblinka
Bergen-Belsen Sachsenhausen Buchenwald
Auschwitz Płaszów Borki Janowska Babi Yar
Kovno Ponary Warsaw Lodz Dachau Ravensbrück
Natzweiler Flossenbürg Fünfteichen Stutthof
Neuengamme Nováky Sered Alderney Szebnie
Skalat Zasów Pustkow Rumbula Lublin Poniatowa
Bogdanovka Vaivara Klooga Karczew Międzyrzec
Nowo-Wilejka Koldyczewo Dworzec Hancewicze
Rozwadow Mielec Trawniki Kaminoka-Strumiłowa
Gross-Rosen Mauthausen Theresienstadt Gusen
Luckenwalde Lieberose Skarżysko-Kamienna
Ebensee Gunskirchen Tuttlingen Fulda Borki
Ohrdruf Nordhausen Dora Gardelegen Minsk
Salzwedel Schorzingen Spaichingen Birkenau
Schömberg Leitmeritz Rehmsdorf Proyanovska
Schlier-Vöcklabruck Chrzanów Bialystok Gurs
Ponar Stanislawów Kolomyja Riga Kaiserwald

~~Polish~~ Jews

hidden in the woods
near Krakow
in Wieliczka, Poland

stands a monument
to the town's
murdered Jews.

an inscription records
the slaughtered
Polish Jews.

somebody has tried
to scratch out the word
Polish.

Facts

The Nazis killed
approximately
two-thirds of all the Jews
living in Europe.

An estimated
1.1 million
Jewish children
were murdered   .
in the Holocaust.

Few survived
the death camps.
For example—
of the 400,000
men, women and children
sent to Chełmno
only 2 came out alive.

Belzec,
where 600,000
men, women and children
were murdered
also had only
2 known survivors.

In addition
to the Jews,
the Nazis murdered
gypsies, homosexuals,
Jehovah's Witnesses,
and the disabled.

Lament

We went as ash to the fields
for fertilizer: we went as ash

to the pond for fill: we went as ash
under the boots of the SS for gravel:

we went as ash and there was nobody
to say Kaddish for us: nobody

but ourselves. In Auschwitz
the guidebook comes in five languages

but it cannot remember our names.

All Jews
Were Criminals
and Subhuman

it did not occur to me
that these orders could be unjust.
I was of the conviction
that all Jews were not innocent but guilty,
that all Jews were criminals and subhuman.
the thought that one should evade
the order to participate
in the extermination of the Jews
did not enter my mind.

From the testimony of Kurt Möbius, former Police Battalion member.

In Your Recurring
Barbed Wire Dream

In your dream
you must put on your old grey stripes
with a hole in the knee,
put on your yellow star and go back.
Back to the *lager*. Back to sleeping on a plank of wood
with six others. Back to washing your face
in morning coffee. Back to *Appell*, the *Kapo*'s blows.
Back to tying your trousers with a piece of string
so the shit won't run out. Back to your number
that is your name—*79584.*

In your dream you smell the stench
like rubber, like flesh burning, burning.
A truck with a large red cross on its side passes.
Stop! you shout. You fling open the back flap,
screaming, screaming—
Where are the children?

In your dream you walk back under the arch.
The words *Arbeit Macht Frei* are burning,
burning like your synagogue, like your Torah.
A baton appears. It points to the tall chimney.
Smoking. Black. Black like the sun.
A voice from a green uniform is laughing, joking:
The showers must be very hot,
the screaming is unusually loud today.

In your dream you are marching out of Auschwitz.
Marching again through snow and sleet.
Through hunger. Cold. Fatigue.
Marching all day, sometimes at night.
Sleeping outside huddled together. Telling yourself
you must not fall behind. You hear the shots.
You see the bodies lying in the ditch.
You see the gutter red with blood.

On frozen feet you are staggering into Dachau,
the SS men greeting you, singing:
Jews go through the Red Sea, waves close in,
the world is happy, Jews are drowned.

SS *Aufseherin* Known for Brutality

Ilsa Koch "The Bitch of Buchenwald"
> had a whip with razor blades which she used on pregnant
> women. She mounted the heads of executed prisoners
> on wooden blocks, made lampshades from inmates'
> tattooed skin.

Irma Grese "The Beautiful Beast"
> whipped and beat prisoners to death and unleashed
> her savage half-starved dogs on the prisoners.

Elisabeth Volkenrath
> oversaw hangings
> and selected prisoners for the gas.

Wanda Klaff
> enjoyed her routine of beating at least two prisoners
> every day.

Elisabeth Lupka
> whipped and beat prisoners while selecting them
> for the gas.

Juana Bormann
> furiously beat sick inmates and unleashed
> her vicious wolfhound on the prisoners.

Dorothea Binz of Ravensbrück
> trained her female guards to be cruel
> and ruthless.

Jenny-Wanda Barkmann "The Beautiful Spectre"
> selected women and children for the gas.
> Known for her cruel treatment and savage
> beating to death of her inmates.

Gerda Steinhoff
>   a ruthless and cruel guard, she selected prisoners
>   for the gas.

Ruth Elfriede Hildner
>   murdered several young female prisoners
>   on a death march.

Ewa Paradies
>   stripped women prisoners naked during the winter,
>   poured ice cold water on them—if a person moved
>   she would beat them.

Ruth Neudeck
>   confessed to cold-blooded murders: like cutting
>   an inmate's throat with a shovel.

Margot Dreschel
>   selected women and children for the gas
>   and beat her inmates brutally.

Maria Mandel "The Beast"
>   enjoyed selecting children to be killed.
>   She was believed to be responsible for the deaths
>   of over 500,000 prisoners in Auschwitz.

Klara Kunig of Ravensbrück
>   was too polite, too kind, and too nice
>   to the women prisoners. She was dismissed
>   and may have been arrested and imprisoned.

Female SS guards were called Aufseherin or female overseers. They were trained in how to punish prisoners and the finer points of Schadenfreude or sadism. Of the 55,000 guards who served in the camps about 3,700 were women.

Mothers

shot burned to death
worked to death
starved to death
asphyxiated on the death trains
raped tortured hanged
beaten to death frozen to death
murdered in their beds
their newborns
thrown out the hospital window
drowned killed by the dogs
died on the wire
walked with their children
to the gas carried babies
in their arms to the gas
O so many mothers
so many many children
who will remember their names?
who will say *Kaddish*
for them?

A Hand or a Head and Terrifying Cries

in Auschwitz,
Marie-Claude Vaillant-Couturier
remembers stacks of corpses
piled up in the courtyard
of Block 25.
she recalls
from time to time
a hand or a head would stir
among the bodies
trying to free itself
and live.

...then there was
that night we were awakened
by terrifying cries—
the following day
we discovered
that the gas supply
had run out—
they had thrown the children
into the furnace
alive.

An Aleph in Treblinka

I'm alone, standing at the edge of a bluff here in Treblinka
just down from a small red shack—was it a guard house?
It's eerily quiet except for a few birds. I look down into
a vast abandoned gravel pit—this was where the Jews
from the forced labor camp called Treblinka I starved
to death, worked to death, as they helped to build
Treblinka II, the extermination camp where over 800,000
mostly Jews met their death. Leaving the gravel pit behind,
I find myself on a long narrow densely forested road
that I hope will lead me to what's left of the main camp.
It's eerily quiet, not a soul in sight. Thinking: this is all
so surreal—nothing so far to indicate the horrors
committed here—I could be walking along a forested road
somewhere in Vermont. Stopping suddenly, I look down
at a small stone under my foot—it's a single Jewish letter
from a chopped up Jewish tombstone—an *Aleph*—
an *Aleph* helping to pave the way to the gas—helping
to pave the way to yet another Jewish graveyard without
headstones, without a *Zayin*, a *Khaf*, a *Mem*—without
a *Shin*, a *Dalet*, a *Gimel*—without an *Aleph* to remember
they had names, they had families, they had a life.

א

Treblinka, 2013

the bodies
doused with diesel fuel and burned
are gone.
gas chambers
that could kill 15,000 people a day
are gone.
no SS, no barbed wire,
no stink.
no one shouts
Tempo Schnell!
no one cries
One Zloty for the baths!
no whips lashing naked Jews
walking to the gas.
no piles of women's hair.
no *Himmelfahrstrasse*,
the road to heaven.

Saved by Chopin

practice all of
Chopin's 24 Études
and they will save you
an inner voice told
Alice Herz-Sommer

and you did—
you played them
all by heart in Terezín
in concert after concert
giving your fellow prisoners
a sense of refuge
and hope

as the transports
came in
and the transports
went out
to somewhere
in the East.

Alice Herz-Sommer gave more than a hundred concerts in Terezín, including twenty
of the complete Chopin Études.

Bomb Auschwitz?

We look up: hundreds of planes—
we want to be bombed, but no bombs.

　　　　—Auschwitz survivor

We hoped to drop our bombs on Auschwitz,
but they wouldn't let us.

　　　　—Lt. Ted Diamond, U.S. Army Airforce

What if the U.S. Army Airforce spared
a couple of leftover bombs
from the war effort,
and instead of dropping them on freight yards,
dumped them
on the crematoriums
after their runs near Auschwitz?
Or what if the RAF ordered some Mosquitoes
to swoop in over the death factory
at low altitude?
Or maybe set up a mission
for Lightning P-38 dive-bombers
to hit the rail lines
of the main deportation routes—
especially the Kosice-Presov railway?
Or what if the War Department
could have been induced
to eat its words:
...the suggested air operation
is impracticable.
Or what if the War Refugee Board
twisted FDR's arm
to open the bomb bay doors over the camp?
Or what if the alarming Vrba-Wetzler report
on what was going on in Auschwitz
alarmed enough naysayers
to send a bunch of 500-pounders
down the tall chimneys?
Then maybe all those Hungarian Jews
deported to the gas in the last months of the war
would have had a chance.

A Few

a few crawled out from the pits under the mass of corpses
       and survived.
a few jumped from the death trains and lived.
a few children were thrown from the death trains
       and died on the tracks.
a few escaped the death camps to tell their story,
       but no one believed them.
a few were hidden by non-Jews who risked their lives
       to save a Jewish life.
a few didn't point a finger to give them away.
a few survived with false papers.
a few married to Aryan spouses survived.
a few fled to the forest joining Jewish partisans
       to fight the Germans.
a few fled to the forest but were hunted down and killed
       by the Poles.
a few, like the Jewish partisan Tuvia Bielski,
       saved the lives of over a thousand of his fellow Jews
       in the forests of Belorussia.
a few tore off their yellow stars
       and slipped under the fence in the ghetto.
a few fought the Germans in the Warsaw ghetto
       before the heavy artillery and flame-throwers got them.
a few led revolts in Treblinka and Sobibor.
a few wanted to bomb Auschwitz.
a few destroyed two of the four gas chambers in Birkenau.
a few, like Bulgaria, refused to deport their Jews
       and managed to save its entire 48,000 Jewish population.
a few, like the English, took children into their homes
       from the *Kindertransport.*
a few, like Raoul Wallenberg, stood up to the Nazis
       and rescued Jews.
a few, like Oskar and Emilie Schindler,
       saved hundreds of Jews from the gas chamber.

a few, like Alice Herz-Sommer,
      lifted the morale and gave hope to her
      fellow prisoners in Terezín by playing
      over a hundred piano concerts.
a few, like Leopold Socha, a Polish sewer worker,
      saved 10 Jews hiding in the dank rat-infested sewers of Lvov.
a few, like the Japanese consul Chiune Sugihara,
      against orders, wrote transit visas
      saving thousands of Jews in Lithuania.
a few, like the German army sergeant Anton Schmid,
      helped smuggle Jews out of Vilna in military trucks.
a few, like the Danes, helped hide & ferry their Jews
      to safety in Sweden.
a few, like Irena Sendler,
      saved the lives of Jewish children
      by smuggling them out of the Warsaw ghetto,
      some of them in coffins.
a few, like Nicholas Winton, set up a rescue operation
      & saved 669 children from Czechoslovakia.
a few, like pastor André Trocomé
      and the people of Le Chambon-sur-Lignon,
      hid Jewish children & adults fleeing the Nazis.
a few, like the four Frieder brothers from Cincinnati—
      Philip, Alex, Morris & Herbert—
      helped 1,200 Jews flee to Manila.
a few, like Dr. Tina Strobos, hid more than 100 Jews
      in an attic in Nazi-occupied Amsterdam just a few blocks
      from the hideout where Anne Frank was captured.
a few, a very few like Peter Bergson, believed the desperate
      situation of the Jews required him to speak out.
      He organized protest rallies, lobbied Congress
      and sought to raise public consciousness about
      the plight of the Jews. His powerful ads like
      Time Races Death: What Are We Waiting For?
      helped raise support to convince President Roosevelt
      to establish the War Refugee Board.

280

a few Jewish refugees labeled "casual baggage"
      were interned behind a fence in Oswego, New York.
a few, like Leon Feldhendler, survived the camps only to be
      murdered by Poles after returning home.
a few, O so few, were saved.

My Son Returns from Auschwitz,

tells me how this oven
made him want to puke

when he saw the firm's name: *Topf*
engraved on the door

like it was some toaster
or oven for your kitchen:

tells me how another name
caught his eye

written on the side
of this battered black bag:

H-E-R-Z
spelling HERZ

his name
and my name

and my grandfather's name
and my grandfather's father's name

and the German name
for heart.

Boxcar 113 0695-5

I am standing outside the Holocaust Museum
      in Madeira Beach, Florida
in front of a lone cattle car
      from Auschwitz.
The sign informs me it is not a cattle car,
      but a boxcar:
            this car has no air slits,
            so it became a suffocation chamber
            for the people, up to 150 at a time
            squeezed into it.
I am running my hands over its slats.
I am climbing the running board the guard rode.
I try the door: it won't slide,
      won't budge.
I see a padlock. Locked. Rusting.
I look for nail holes.
I look up:
      the palm tree is a tall chimney
      belching red and black.
Stench of burning flesh. Shouting. Crying.
      Dogs bark. Loudspeakers blare.
Guard towers. Barbed wire stretches to the horizon.
I am jumping down.
A strange skeleton in stripes is whispering
      in my ear:
Say you're eighteen.
Tell them you have a trade.

Waiting

in Auschwitz/Birkenau
among the
burned-down foundations
they called Canada,*
I stumble upon
a small heap
of bent forks & spoons
& knives—

thinking—
they've been waiting,
rusting & waiting
for the *Shabbat* table
to be set,
for the candles
to be lit,
for the blessing
to be recited,

for the wine
to be sipped,
for the *Challa*
to be shared—
waiting & waiting
for seventy years now
for the *Shabbat* dinner
that will never come.

Canada: where they sorted & stored the victims' belongings before sending them on to the Reich.

On Looking at a Suitcase with a Broken Strap
Holocaust Museum, DC

did you pack it
like they told you:

two dresses for summer
two dresses for winter

and whatever else
you can carry?

look, your name:

Worch
Eva

your birthday:

geb
6V29

your *Judentransport*:

X794

still there
in bold white letters

on the side
where they told you:

so it shouldn't get lost
mark it.

Don't Touch

I shift my shoes and soup bowl under my head,
dream I eat a turnip, the camp bell rings,

rings every dark morning at four, sometimes three:
a voice shouts *Aufstehen,* get up! *Appell! Appell!*

stand in the cold, freezing at the morning roll call:
I am washing my face in morning coffee:

I am tying my trousers at the bottom with a piece
of string so the shit won't run out:

my wooden shoes slip in the mud, the stench of the
cremo strong today: *links, links, links und links:*

marching out under the arch with my *Kommando,*
out under the sign: *Arbeit Macht Frei*

I am running my hands over the rough wooden planks
of my dark three-tiered bunk in my barracks

in the Holocaust Museum in DC
I'm reading the sign: *Don't Touch.*

Marked

For Anita Schorr

at nine
you wore the yellow star,
the Star of David
that marked you *Jew,*
marked you for the cattle car,
marked you for Terezín, for Bergen-Belsen,
marked you for Auschwitz
where you lost your name
for a number—
71569

will the tall chimney roar?
will it belch its stench red and black?
will you go to the showers
that aren't showers?
will you stand without falling
through the long *Appells?*
will you avoid the dogs, the *kapo*'s blows?
will they take your number
at the next *selektion?*

a girl of fourteen
you say you're eighteen
like your mother tells you,
hiding your undeveloped body,
slipping out of Mengele's hands,
out of Auschwitz
into Hamburg slave labor,
a red stripe down your back,
the errant bomb burying you,
the German soldier
pulling you out, befriending you,
giving you half his sandwich
every day

until the day the cattle car dumps you
into Bergen-Belsen,
into the living dead, the walking dead:
and the flesh of the dead
some are eating
before the British are coming,
and you tell yourself:
I'm going to make it!
willing yourself to survive,
to bear witness
for all of those who lost their names
who lost their lives
simply because
they were marked
like you:
Jew

At the Sound of the Siren

at ten in the morning
in Israel

at the
sound of the siren

everyone stops
what they're doing

cars pull over
and stop

everyone stands silent
in remembrance

Yom HaShoah

Old Survivors Dying

the old Holocaust survivors are dying.
      here, in America & around the world
          they are dying & dying.
the ones who were marked with the star.
the ones who were marked with a number for a name.
the ones who survived the round-ups
          the terror of the ghettos
          the death trains.
the ones in hiding who weren't betrayed & survived.
the ones who lived as a hunted animal & survived.
the ones whose children were torn from them & "sent away."
the ones whose parents were shot in front of them.
the ones who fought for life surrounded by death.
the ones in the camps who never would have made it
          without someone's help.
the ones whose father, mother, brothers & sisters,
          grandmother & grandfather
          were all gassed on arrival at Auschwitz.
the ones who cheated the Nazis & rode the *Kindertransport*
          to a safe haven in England,
          but never saw their parents again.
old survivors now—their ranks thinning out
          dying & dying.
the ones who survived the selections.
the ones who lived with the smell of corpses & diarrhea
          & saw their comrades dying.
the ones who lived with the rats darting back & forth
          devouring the naked corpses.
the ones whose bodies were stained with blood
          from the dog's fangs.
the ones who walked back from work
          dragging their comrades' dead corpses.
the ones who were covered with lice,
          living in mud
          on a starvation diet.

the ones who emptied the trucks
                & threw the still warm bodies
                   into the graves.
the ones who couldn't cry anymore.
the ones who fought hunger, thirst, abuse, fatigue & despair,
                but didn't throw themselves on the wire.
the ones who saw men, women & children being led to the gas.
the ones who nearly froze to death
                but survived the death marches.
the ones who can't forget the indifference of the onlookers
                & the silence of those
                   believed to be one's friends.
the ones who had neither homes nor families
                     nor countries to return to.
the ones who never discovered
                what happened to their loved ones.
the ones who lived with & overcame
                the pain & the nightmares.
the ones with traumatic wounds who still have sleepless nights.
the ones who can never ever forget the stench of burning flesh.
the ones who came back from the dead but are still there.
the ones who keep asking themselves
                "why am I alive when six million died?"
the ones without a single person left in the world
          who went on to build a new family, a new life.
the old survivors,
       in their youth then
             in their eighties now—
you've read their memoirs,
           seen their Spielberg interviews—
in the schools, the churches, the synagogues,
              you've heard their poignant voices—
voices of living history
        that thrust us into the midst of things,
            that give history a human face—

the voices fading, fading
                  like their blue tattoos—
as *never forget* grows more important with each passing year,
         who will be left to deny the deniers?
who will be left to speak for the dead burnt bodies,
              to carry on for every one of their lost ones'
                        unfinished lives?
who will be left
        to rescue the dead from oblivion?

Auschwitz, 2013

no chimney belching
red and black

no stink

no SS no *Kapo* no *Häftling*
no *Muselmann*

no orchestra's
dying notes

no Mengele
no *selektion*

no whistles no shots
no cries from Block 25

no one stands *appell*
no one goes on the wire

green grass

if we had grass
we would've eaten it

by the pond
of ashes

cattail spikes bend
in the wind

like arms waving
waving

over the gate iron words
still mock us

Arbeit Macht Frei

Let There Be Remembrance

For Zelig Preis

let there be remembrance

in our souls in our hearts

let our hearts bleed

for those who perished

let the perished

be more than a statistic

let the statistic have a face

let the face have a voice

let the voice cry out to us

through the time

let the time

be remembered

through the years

let the years

never ever

forget.

Stephen Herz's poems have been widely published. He's a winner of the New England Poet's Daniel Varoujan Prize. This collection—*Marked*—is the culmination of two chapbooks, a volume of poems—*Whatever You Can Carry*—and many new poems that cover the years of this dark, bloody time of death and destruction and evil we call the Holocaust or Shoah. Several schools and universities have adopted Herz's poems as part of their Holocaust studies curricula. Mr. Herz lives in Westport, CT and New York City.

www.ingramcontent.com/pod-product-compliance
Lightning Source LLC
Chambersburg PA
CBHW022005080426
42733CB00007B/474